Blueprint for Growth

Lessons on Life, Ministry and Leadership for Young Christian Leaders

Tim King

Blueprint for Growth

First published by Westbow Press 2014. Copyright © Tim King, Blueprint for Growth; 21 Transformational steps to help your church grow to its full potential.

This 2nd edition published in 2020 by Elluminet Press Ltd - www.elluminetpress.com.

"Pastor Tim is a man who wants you to succeed—succeed in who you are in Christ and succeed in the mission that God has called you to do. He is a man who will help you grow and achieve your potential in Christ. This book is a mixture of inspiration—you can do it, yet it is laced with the practical—how can you do it? If you are starting a church for the first time or just want to make sure you have thought through what you are doing, this book is for you!"

—Pastor Ed Carter, Valley Church, Preston, United Kingdom

"In this book, Tim's heart and passion come through to see great churches and great leaders be all they can be!"

—Pastor John Greenow, Xcel Church, Newton Aycliffe, United Kingdom

"Tim King has passion, giftedness, and ability in Christian communication capable of delivering in a wide range of situations. His hands-on approach will enhance churches' needs in training and in motivating Christian growth and mission engagement. I recommend Tim to you as an energetic and very able Christian minister."

—Dr. John C. Douglas, Sage Resources, Tauranga, New Zealand

"Tim has a love and regard for the local church; his inspirational and in-depth delivery will open the minds of his listeners and ignite a hunger for more of God."

—Don McDonell, Senior Pastor, Inspire Church, Auckland, New Zealand

As always, to my wife, Penny, and to our six daughters. Without their support, nothing could be accomplished. And to those leaders I admire and follow: Don McDonell and Mike Hadwin in New Zealand. Their inspiration and character have meant much to me over the last few years.

Table of Contents

Foreword

This book is a heartfelt and passionate cry for contemporary churches and Christian leaders to be all they can be. It is a practical handbook, containing some great guidelines and suggestions born from Tim King's wealth of experience and observations in leadership—both within the church and the secular marketplace.

As a pastor and leader, I believe you will find this book helpful in your journey of leadership and ministry.

Pastor John Greenow
Xcel Church, County Durham
United Kingdom

Acknowledgements

Many people have helped me develop my understanding of leadership over the years. There are far too many people to name but thank you anyway.

I'd like to offer a special thanks to the following individuals:

I am grateful to Dr. Ian Jagelman of the Jagelman Institute, Australia, who helped light the fire inside of me. Because of him, I see that ministry builds people but leadership can build great churches.

My gratitude also extends to Don MacDonell, of Inspire Church, New Zealand, who has such great faith and who is a phenomenal evangelist. He helped me see that winning the lost for Christ is the main mission of the church.

These two men have helped me shape my own purpose, which is to build men and women to become great leaders so that they may build great churches to reach the lost for the cause of Christ.

Additional gratitude goes to the late Dave Holding, who has been a great friend since my arrival here in the United Kingdom. He believed in what I could do. His prayer and support were a constant in an all but perfect journey.

And last but not least, I am deeply thankful for my lovely and very patient wife, Penny, without whose help, encouragement, and the occasional proverbial kick in the rear end, nothing would have been accomplished.

Preface to 2nd Edition

The hardest thing for any author to do is to hand his or her manuscript over to a publisher; it is like handing over your child to a complete stranger. After it is published you then start to think about the things you didn't say or thought you needed to say, but never got round to writing. Earlier this year, as the world groaned under the Covid 19 restrictions and many were told to stay at home, I had an opportunity to revisit Blueprint for Growth, first published in 2014.

At the heart of my ministry I have always had young believers, or young pastors and leader's front and centre in my thoughts. I have always endeavoured to answer their questions. I have always been concerned that they have as many answers as possible, before they go out into the work of God. I don't want them to make the same mistake I and many thousands before them have made.

This book is just that an attempt to look at those things that the young pastor or Christian leader have not learned at Bible College or Seminary. It is an attempt to ensure that they are prepared and that they won't be ambushed before they even get started.

A person learns to walk by taking one step at a time. A pastor cannot go into God's work with a theological degree; they need a calling a true calling. Through this book I have tried to help the young pastor by answering the questions of life, ministry and leadership in the church, and to do it one step at a time.

Tim King

Oxford

Christmas 2020

Introduction

Introduction

Is it presumptuous for this book to claim that I can make your church grow? Or pose the questions, thoughts and ideas that are generally not discussed at Bible College or seminary.

Sitting on the shelf in my local bookshop's self-help section is a plethora of books competing to provide advice to an avid readership on how they might improve their lives. Topics range from marriage, sex, and dating to business and finance, and from how to exercise and eat well to how to deal with a demanding toddler. Who hasn't been tempted to read at least the back cover of a book claiming to disclose an ancient tropical formula for burning off some amount of bodyweight per week? I especially love the books promising to reveal the ten best-kept secrets of how to get rich—after the reader has posted a ten-dollar check!

When you move to the Christian bookshelf, you find books covering an equally diverse range of subjects and genres: inspiring autobiographies of great mega-church leaders, how-to books on the laws and principles of leadership, and devotionals and books on spiritual truth. You'll find books on the second coming of Christ and books exploring various schools of thought about the end times. There is one area, however, where the selection of books is likely to be slim: books discussing how to grow your church. Those you do find might tell you what has worked for one particular person or church, but rarely do these books expound upon the principles and underlying ideas that make a given approach applicable to other settings. You will also find that because of the desire to appear positive, these books rarely share what didn't work or how many times the author failed before succeeding!

In this book, I intend to fill that gap—to offer a Christian self-help book that will help your own leadership, pose questions that you may have asked yourself but confined them to the too hard basket, give you ideas and help your church grow as well as tell you what won't work. This book spells out the hard work ahead of you and the significant cultural changes required to make your church a success.

In 1982, I had the privilege to visit my friend Gary at Christ for the Nations Institute Bible college, in Dallas, Texas. This was my first trip to the United States, and I was excited to see how the college operated. I had heard such good reports, and in comparison, my own college had been dull and boring. One evening at a youth meeting, the leader stood up and said, "Let's sing the cockroach song." Laughter erupted, and music started. With great gusto, the young people (about 1,500 of them) sang these words:

"They rush on the city, they run on the walls, for great is the army that carries out God's Word."

It struck me afresh in that moment that the church is purposed to be a vast army advancing rapidly and taking ground with direction and focus. Those young people passionately believed that in singing these words they would extend and take forward the kingdom of God. Today (nearly forty years later), we are constantly being told by the world's media that the church is in decline. Many claim that Christianity is no longer relevant and has no bearing on the way people live. I dispute this! I see that the church worldwide is growing, is still relevant, and still has a purpose for today's society. However, many (not all) Christian leaders have lost focus and forgotten their purpose. Many of those leaders are still using antiquated ideas to try to grow their churches and then wonder why their churches don't grow. Christian leaders have become so cocooned in their Christianity that they no longer understand what is happening in their communities or in ordinary people's lives.

I had been in church ministry for about five years when I decided to resign and, for a time, pursue a secular career path. I left a relatively successful youth pastorate for a number of reasons. First, I had come into ministry straight from Bible college, which had not prepared me for ministry. In fact, it taught me nothing about real life! Second, I felt I needed to gain work experience in order to understand what most people experience in their everyday lives (I realized that church life for a minister can be very sheltered). Third, I was tired of the excuses people made to explain why their churches were not growing. I was the youth pastor of a church that was growing rapidly; in an eighteen-month period, youth participation went from four young people to about seventy. I couldn't understand why other churches weren't growing. I asked myself why they were not seeing growth. Was I doing something different? Lastly, I pursued the secular path because I wanted to earn a decent salary that kept me fed instead of just humble!

As I progressed through the ranks of management and into running my own business, I developed management and leadership skills that were sorely lacking in the church: strategic planning, skills development such as sales and marketing skills, people skills, learning to read people and understand body language as well as communication, vision setting, forecasting—all skills to help an organization or business grow and keep on growing. Also, I learned people skills, including how to hire good staff and fire bad staff and how to avoid feeling threatened by people who knew more than I did. These are practical skills not usually taught to young leaders in churches or in Bible colleges, but they are vital when growing a business. I had to ask myself why these very same skills could not be translated and transferred into a church setting.

I have to point out here that I do not believe that churches are businesses. However, good management practice and great leadership skills are evidence of a healthy vibrant church. When you go to these churches across the globe there is a tangible presence of excellence in the way its message is presented.

Let us remember, as someone once said, "The church is God's plan A; he doesn't have a plan B."[1] We are preaching the resurrected Christ to a dying world, and as such, we need to present ourselves in the best possible light, without compromise. A shoddy, ill-disciplined, and chaotic Sunday morning service is not the way to do it. Whenever church leaders speak to me about church growth, they often ask if I'm being presumptuous by claiming I can make their church grow. I qualify my statement by quoting two Scriptures from the Bible:
"It's not by Might or by power but by my Spirit says the Lord" and "a grain of wheat falls to the ground and all by itself it grows, first the stalk then the ear" (Zechariah 4:6; Mark 4:28 KJV). Nobody alone can make any church grow—neither I nor any church leader.

---

1   Dwight Robertson, *You are God's Plan A: There Is No Plan B* (Colorado Springs: David C. Cook, 2010).

Only God can make a church grow.

So am I being presumptuous in saying I can make your church grow? Or to prompt you to think about how you do things, I don't think so! The skills and leadership principles that I have learned in different countries, such as Zimbabwe, South Africa, New Zealand, Australia, and the United Kingdom, have put me in good stead. Also, the time I have spent observing churches and church leaders in different denominations, both Pentecostal and evangelical, my years as a youth pastor and pastor, uniquely positions me to see just where a church or church organization is failing. The steps, ideas and prompts I will share in the following chapters are practical, helpful, and relevant to your church and its position in the community you serve. If these things are put into practice and used by you and your leadership team (if you have one), they will result in growth. They will also enhance your leadership and will help develop your ministry.

When I was a boy, I helped a neighbor build a hothouse in his garden (a hothouse is similar to a greenhouse but is built partly underground). I did so because I had never seen one being built and also to supplement my meager pocket money! First, we dug a trench about four feet deep and wide enough for two people to pass each other. Then we built two brick walls inside of the trench and stone steps leading out of it. The walls were two bricks higher that the surrounding ground level. Next, we built a frame to surround the trench, but it was a few feet wider (the sides were about eighteen inches high). We nailed bits of old tin and aluminum sheeting onto this frame. On top, we built a lightweight pitched roof, and we nailed chicken mesh and clear plastic sheeting to it. Inside the hothouse we spread well-rotted compost up to the level of the bricks and prepared the soil for plants and seedlings. During the day it got very hot, and then at night it would stay a lot warmer than the outside temperatures. As a result, my neighbor could grow out of season flowers and other such plants all year. He had created the right environment and atmosphere for growth.

How do we make our churches grow? We make a plan, we create

a framework from that plan, we get help where required, and we purposefully create an atmosphere in which the church can grow. Just like any gardener, we build the greenhouse to create the right atmosphere—to encourage growth and multiplication. It has been said that church leaders should be thermostats, not thermometers. We should be the people setting the temperature, not the ones reading it.

While on my travels around the world, I have met hundreds of church leaders and pastors who struggle to get their churches to grow. Most have congregations of 40 to 50 members. Others can't seem to get beyond the 180 mark or the 300 to 350 range. All of them desperately want to keep their congregations growing, spreading the message of Christ, but they've seemingly hit invisible road blocks or else watched their numbers decline. There are valid reasons why churches of these sizes stagnate. This book will help those leaders overcome obstacles, and in so doing, build fruitful and dynamic congregations. For our part, much depends on what we are prepared to do to get there and what sacrifices we are prepared to make. The rest we leave to God.

Finally, let me say what this book is not. It is not a book with rules and laws. It does not deal with theories of leadership or what makes a leader tick. It's not about examining where we're going wrong and sitting back in defeat. This book is about learning practical and positive skills to help us do what Jesus said we should do— go and make disciples. This book is a book of ideas to challenge thought processes and to get us to ask ourselves questions about how we do church. This book is about helping us to fulfill the Great Commission. It's about creating a successful, relevant, and mission-focused church.

This book is about doing real life together.

1

Emotional Intelligence: The Psychology of Christian Leadership

Chapter 1: Emotional Intelligence

Step One: Emotional Intelligence

Some years ago I read a great book called On the Psychology of Military Incompetence.[1] The book recounts several famous military blunders and examines why those responsible (some of Britain's greatest generals) failed. These generals were responsible for some of the greatest military defeats ever to occur in the history of warfare. For example, General Redvers Buller led the British forces at the start of the Boer War in South Africa at the turn of the twentieth century. Buller had, as a young officer, won the Victoria Cross—the highest military honor awarded by the British Army—and was loved by the public and by many of his subordinates. However, the higher in rank he rose, the more incompetent he became. He grossly underestimated the Boer generals and their men. He viewed them in the same light as the Zulu tribesmen he had encountered previously during the Anglo Zulu campaigns of the 1870's. Buller suffered some humiliating defeats, but instead of employing new tactics or gathering new information, he continued to fail, all because he would not change. He was eventually replaced, and the tide of the war turned. The author of the book goes on to question how these extremely efficient, popular, and highly decorated men ended up in such desperate circumstances: their armies defeated, themselves forlorn, and their careers ruined.

Over the last few years, since reading this book, I have had reason to ask the same question of myself and of many church leaders and pastors I have encountered. There are multiple reasons why any of these leaders may have failed. Fundamentally, however, their shortcomings emerge from an inability to relate to, respond to, and react with other people. This can be known as emotional intelligence, or EQ. EQ is the ability to be aware of the feelings and emotions of others and to use these effectively for the benefit of all concerned. EQ is the outward manifestation of all that we have learned, it is who we are, it is how others perceive us. The best example I have of a Christian leader operating with poor EQ is in the below story about Pastor John.

---

1   Norman Dixon, *On the Psychology of Military Incompetence* (London: Pimlico, 1976).

First, however, here is some useful background information. If you aimed to buy or sell a property in New Zealand, you would eventually reach a point in the process where the term going unconditional would be applied. This occurs when both parties are in a position to commit, and the finances are in place. You would sign the document and "go unconditional" on an agreed upon date. Once signed, the document protects both the buyer and the seller, and no one signs it if there are likely to be any problems.

Well, Pastor John had a successful church; it was one of the largest in his city and continued to grow rapidly. However, Pastor John felt that the building was growing too small for the congregation. Also, it was old and not in keeping with the image he wanted for his church. He believed that God wanted him to sell it and purchase a new, modern building, and he had found just the place! With the consent of his leadership, he entered negotiations to purchase the new building. However, he also put the old building on the market without his leadership knowing.

Pastor John wanted to step out in faith, so he signed the document to go unconditional on a specific date. He didn't yet have the finances in place, but he believed the bank would happily provide the money he needed for a mortgage. After all, he was a leading citizen of the city, he knew both the mayor and the bank manager personally, and he was sure the old building would sell quickly. All this he did without telling his leadership.

Unfortunately, he had failed to foresee the collapse of the international banks (brought about by the subprime lending debacle in the United States). The collapse triggered a worldwide recession that impacted many banks both in the United States and around the globe, including in New Zealand. The banks stopped lending money for a time. To add to the problem, the old building failed to attract a buyer—it was not in a prime location. Pastor John had a legal obligation to meet the requirements of the document he had signed. If he did not, he would lose the new and the old building as well as owe massive amounts of money to cover the legal costs incurred. He grew increasingly worried but did not go to anyone for help for some time.

Eventually, he approached another pastor who had recently purchased a modern building. He was told, in no uncertain terms, to tell someone immediately, to seek advice from the businesspeople in his church, and to approach his lawyers. Frustratingly, Pastor John did none of these things. The day for going unconditional arrived, and the ugly mess rapidly unfolded.

The main problem in this story is that Pastor John operated with a complete lack of EQ. He felt his own life experience would help him through the problems, his inner self told him to trust himself rather than rely on and trust others. He failed to communicate his intentions clearly and made huge decisions based on what he alone felt God was saying. His judgments were not made on the basis of knowledge or common sense; nor did he consider the wider implications of his actions. Sadly, he failed to ask the right questions until it was too late. He didn't act upon the advice given from someone more experienced or respond to the changing situation; instead, he alienated his leaders by deciding he could manage the situation himself. As a result, the leadership team lost all confidence in their pastor, which led to the collapse of the church, a large legal bill, disrepute for the wider movement, and the loss of the new building. Pastor John lost his job and his reputation.

I have the utmost respect for pastors who can build and maintain a congregation of 150. It's a great achievement. However, this number is built solely upon the pastor's individual capabilities and ministry gifting. Many are satisfied and seem happy to go through their pastoral career having had a modicum of success. But why stop there? By employing some simple leadership techniques, pastors can increase and fill their EQ tanks. EQ can be learned and developed through life experience, listening to others. Pastors can build on their leadership abilities, and see their congregations double to 300 to 350 in size, if not even more. Below I have listed four common pitfalls we must avoid as church leaders in order to see real and positive changes happen in our congregations:

Fundamental Conservatism

On a well-known social media site, a friend of mine lamented the fact that too many churches were using strobe lights, smoke machines, loud music, and professional worship bands to build their congregations. There was not enough "good old-fashioned preaching" or Holy Spirit ministry. I must confess to thinking his words belied a tinge of jealousy after a lack of success in his own ministry. However, I also believe that his own conservatism had prevented him from seeing the whole picture. I belong to one of these churches he describes. It is a vibrant, joyous, relevant, people-focused, and fast growing church. While it has all the things my friend mentioned, it also has Bible-centered preaching and an appeal for people to commit their lives to Christ after every Sunday service. So what is the difference between us? Put simply, my friend is ministry-focused, whereas my own church is leadership-focused. His fundamental conservative background (the same as my own, I might add) prevents him from putting aside outworn traditions and profiting from the successful experiences of others. Our beliefs are the same, and these are not negotiable for either of us. Holy-Spirit-led ministry does indeed build people, but leadership (not ministry) builds the church. We need both.

A Tendency to Overestimate One's Abilities

Many pastors, such as Pastor John, do too much with little understanding or expertise. Ministry is different from leadership. Your ministry is what helps you pray for people; it helps and defines your preaching and its success; it is the Holy-Spirit-driver that sees you long for the lost to come to Christ. Ministry is not your ability to influence others or to facilitate their ministries, and it is not building relationships to develop other people's abilities—that is leadership. Leadership skills are increased when we make an effort to increase our own intellectual abilities and to increase our life skills (EQ). Church leaders and pastors often fail because we overestimate our own abilities in these areas; at the same time, we do nothing to develop ourselves. For example, I am always amazed at how little pastors read about current affairs or modern cultural trends in their own communities. I am also amazed at how many leaders rely on their own ability to preach well rather than focus time and energy on developing the preaching abilities of others.

Often we rely solely on our own areas of ministry to get the job done and forget the experience and abilities of others.

A Focus on Problems, Not the Vision

Many of the generals in Dixon's book failed because they lost sight of their objective. They became distracted and began to blame others or had capable officers removed (and often replaced by less capable men). In an effort to solve every problem, they lost their focus on the primary objective. Church leaders fail because rather than focus on the vision, they focus on the problems. Instead of empowering capable people to fix these problems, they become embroiled in the problem-solving process. Often, such behavior results from a lack of intellectual ability or an unwillingness to learn and develop (as mentioned previously). Life experience has not prepared them to deal with some situations. Rather than go around or over a problem, they prefer to bang their heads against its wall! People leave churches not usually because of a difference in doctrine but because of fundamental differences in philosophy, something that a pastor says or a way that he acts. However, things change when everyone is focused on one vision and its objectives with an "all in it together" attitude. The whole group owns problems so that individuals with the right expertise can problem-solve rather than relying on one individual leader and his or her weaknesses.

Indecisiveness and an Abdication of Leadership

A leader should not abdicate their position because of pressure from others. The leader should lead! Be decisive even if you don't have all the facts, and don't second-guess yourself—make your decision and stick to it (you can always adapt as time goes on). Indecisiveness can lead to uncertainty, which makes others feel uncomfortable. Even if the right decision is made, people learn not to trust you. This can result in becoming paranoid about one's leadership position, which will lead to eventually self-destruction. To avoid this scenario, remember that it's okay to fail. People don't expect perfection, but they do expect confidence, truthfulness and decisiveness. That being said, don't forget to balance your decisiveness against the relationships you are building. Self-centeredness destroys; it never builds. If you find yourself trying to cover your own back or following your own agenda (of benefit primarily to you), it may be that self-centeredness has crept in.

Summary and Checklist

Our beliefs are fundamental to *who* we are, not *how* we worship God. Life experience has shaped us in a particular way. The skills we have developed have not only increased our intellectual capacity but increased our emotional capacity (EQ) as well. Neither is our emotional intelligence static we can continually learn and develop this area of our lives. Let us also remember that our own conservatism revolves around what we believe, not just what we wear or the music we sing.

Consider the following:

- Look at trends around you, and without compromise assess if your church structure, service, or attitudes need updating.

- Build communication networks with your church leaders so you can meet regularly. Trust them to do their part.

- Practice decision making: it will gradually increase your confidence.

- Increase your skills: ministry doesn't stop when you leave Bible college; leadership development does not either. (This idea will be discussed in more detail in chapter 14.)

- Ask yourself why you do what you do. Is it because of the way you have been brought up? Is it a reflection of your emotional intelligence? Is it because you have always done church in a particular way?

- Never stand still. Always grow. Always move forward.

- Go to chapter two to learn the second step!

2

Why Do People Go into Ministry?

Chapter 2: Why Do People Go into Ministry?

Step Two: Consider Why You Went into Ministry

From time to time, I have encountered people who believe me to be against all church leadership. Their perception is that I frequently cast it in a bad light. Ironically, there is nothing further from the truth; I am extremely in favor of good church leadership. That being said, I have come across some very poor church leadership on my travels. If some of these leaders had instead been managing directors of secular companies, they would have either gone into liquidation or been fired by the board!

On British television, there is a genealogy program called "Who Do You Think You Are?" The format has also been copied for television in the United States. On the show, celebrities research their family trees and find all the skeletons in the closets. I like the title because it is a question I ask of church leaders. I ask, "Who do you think you are? What makes you think you can do a better job than those who have gone before you?"

I often have the privilege of meeting one-on-one with a church leader who wants help or advice. One of the first things I ask is *why* they went into church leadership in the first place. Below are some of the most common responses, which I have found rather interesting:

- God called me into ministry.

- I've always felt this is what I should do.

- I come from a family of preachers.

- I have a yearning to see souls won for Christ.

- I am God's answer to the problems in this town.

- I went to Bible college—what else should I do?

Before we continue, I would like to point out that every Christian is called into ministry. We are all called to spread the gospel, to evangelize and to make disciples of humankind.

Every church leader I come across has a ministry. Examples include preaching, teaching, providing pastoral care, evangelizing, or leading worship (to name but a few). Perhaps you can identify with more than one ministry area in this list, or possibly you can even add to it. However, my question was not "Why did you go into church ministry?" but rather, "Why did you go into church leadership?"

A church growth and leadership guru once said, "Ministry builds people but leadership builds churches."[1] The reason some church leaders fail is they don't understand the difference between ministry and leadership. For example, I believe I am called to lead a church, but I am not called to pastor a church. Unfortunately, this sort of statement would not win me many invites to lead churches, because recruiting boards often muddle the two. They think that ministry and leadership are one and the same. They are not.

Ephesians 4:11 tells us that one of the gifts set in the church by the Holy Spirit is the gift of pastoring. Romans 12:8 shows us that the Holy Spirit likewise gives the gift of leadership to the church. These Scriptures complement one another. They demonstrate the diversity of the work of the Holy Spirit within the church.

It is indeed possible for someone to be the leader of a church without being a gifted pastor, teacher, or evangelist. John Maxwell says, "Leadership is influence,"[2] but I think that Ian Jagelman (of the Jagelman Institute in Australia) puts it better when he says, "Leadership is an activity which directs influences and facilitates ministry in others."[3] But I believe that great leadership accomplishes these things while simultaneously building relationships with people. We should never forget that church leadership is all about people! It's about how we direct people, how we influence them, how we activate their gifting, how we facilitate their ministries, and how we build relationships with them.

A few months ago, I sat down with a young couple that had been

---

1   Ian Jagelman, *The Empowered Church* (Adelaide, Australia: Openbooks, 1998).

2   John C. Maxwell, *The 21 Irrefutable Laws of Leadership* (Thomas Nelson, 2007). Chapter 2The Law of Influence. Page 11

3   Ian Jagelman, *The Empowered Church* (Adelaide, Openbooks 1998). Chapter 1 The distinction between ministry and leadership page 9.

pastoring a church for seven years. They were depressed, rundown, and stressed out because of church life. I opened my conversation with my two questions, "Why are you in church leadership?" and "What makes you think you can do a better job than those who came before you?" The man responded that ministry was something he had always wanted to do and explained that his father, uncle, and brother were all "in the ministry" too. Next, I asked his wife why she wanted to be in leadership, and immediately she burst into tears. Through the sobs she confessed that while she wanted to support her husband, she did not wish to be in any sort of leadership or ministry. It was too painful and was taking a toll on her children, her marriage, and her attitude toward those in the congregation. I looked at her husband and asked him in which area of ministry he felt he was gifted. His reply, "in pastoring," came without hesitation. From that moment, the way forward for this couple seemed clear to me. I advised them to find a church where he could be number two instead of number one, which would release him to serve as a pastor instead of as the senior leader. Unsurprisingly, he was a little taken aback by the finality of my answer! He made it clear to me that he did not want to move on.

Before our meeting, I had gathered information about this couple's church. When they took over, it had had a congregation of around fifteen older people, and it had grown to approximately fifty people within the past seven years. Of this fifty, twenty people had followed the pastor from his old church, ten people had either moved into the area or returned to church when they heard there was a new pastor, and five people were new converts. The average age of the congregation was fifty-two (although there were seven older teenagers). The local parish had a population of around twenty-five thousand and was served by two high schools and two primary schools. While his vision was to reach the lost for Christ, this man had no clear strategy on how to accomplish it. A small Sunday school, run by his wife, met on Sunday afternoons at the local community hall. There was no youth program, and he was not sure how to use his existing young people to establish one. The music group was made up of talented congregation members who resembled a sixties rock band! The music being sung was from the 1980s and '90s to accommodate the older congregation. Indeed, when I talked to the congregation members, they all felt that the young pastor did a great job meeting their needs in visitation, prayer, and good preaching.

Because the young man did not wish to move or give up his pastorate here, in short, are the suggestions I made to this couple:

1. Start again. Look for a more permanent venue to call home. The current venue was a local community hall and after a Saturday night a great deal of time was spent on the clean up on a Sunday. A new more permanent venue would give his congregation a sense of wellbeing and security.

2. Change the name of the church. In the Bible when God wanted to do a new thing He changed the name of a person. Or the people of Israel renamed the place to reflect what God had done there. For example; "The First Baptist Church of Deadwood" could be changed to "Deadwood Christian Life Center" to better reflect the ethos and culture of a church and the new direction it was taking.

3. Change the meeting time to Sunday mornings.

4. Appoint an older young person to lead the youth work, and help this individual develop a strategy of outreach into the local schools.

5. Learn new songs that are more youth-appropriate, and encourage the teens to learn musical instruments.

6. Create a pastoral care team to take on the everyday pastoral needs of the congregation. Home groups are the 'front line' of pastoral care, so choose leaders that have good pastoral gifts.

7. Get a clear idea of where the church should be in ten years, and start to plan the move forward to make it happen.

8. Change the preaching style from purely exposition to also covering topical and relevant issues.

9. Frequently refer people back to the vision and strategy. In doing so, you give others the chance to catch the vision and, crucially, gain an understanding of how they can be part of making it happen.

10. Visit and have coffee with church leaders who are succeeding in other churches. Build a relationship with them, and after some time invite them to come speak to your leaders.

11. Take a holiday.

My aim was to encourage the young pastor to focus on leadership development and strategy, not primarily his pastoral ministry. With this focus, he could achieve great things. However, if he would rather solely develop his pastoral gifting, my initial advice, it would indeed be better for him to seek a position in another church as an assistant pastor. He needed to learn to influence others rather than try to do everything himself. He had to learn to trust others to do the job! At the same time I encouraged his wife to see herself as a partner and that she too should learn to delegate and only do the things where she felt she could make a difference, in everything else she should protect her family.

In summary, you can put a square peg in a round hole—you will need a large mallet and brute force! It can be painful, but church pastors need to set aside their ministry at the appropriate time in order to lead and give direction in order to facilitate ministries and to release others. They need to learn to put the right people in the right place. In doing so, senior leaders create for themselves precious space to fulfill the roles only they can fulfill: to seek the face of God for direction and vision and to lead their church into that vision.

Leading a church is a vocation and a calling. With it comes an awesome responsibility to enable the church to grow. If you imagine that you alone are God's answer to your town—find a different job! If you're fresh out of Bible college looking for a church—stop and get a different job first! If you are going into ministry because your family is all involved, no problem—but take time to examine your motives first. Church is a hard taskmaster, and many young men and women have been destroyed by it. When I went into the church fulltime, I was sure of God's call on my life.

Nonetheless, I've made huge mistakes along the way (and almost been destroyed by these). Praise God, I learned that leadership, not just ministry, was the key. Our God is not a God of small things, and so those who say they prefer quality over quantity (in terms of church membership) are on the wrong track or making excuses for their own inadequacies in leadership. We need quality *and* quantity in order to see the church influence our communities, towns, counties, and nations.

Summary and advice checklist

It is essential for anybody going into church ministry or Christian leadership to be sure of their call and the reasons that they go into this line of work.

- Honestly assess why you chose to go into the church as an occupation.

- Understand the difference between your ministry gifting and your position as a leader.

- Ask yourself whether you have the right people in the right places. If not, make changes.

- Never go into church ministry/leadership without the full, unequivocal support of your wife or husband.

3

Should You Lead
Someone Else's Church?

Step Three: Ask Yourself If You Should Lead Someone Else's Church

For quite some time, I've been mentally mulling over the concept of church planting versus the idea of taking on an existing church (church placement). I have concluded that my bias is toward church planting, which we will take a good look at it in the following chapter. First, however, let's examine the issues surrounding church placement, which usually happens when a denomination places you in a particular church or when you are invited to take on an already existing pastorate.

Over the last six months or so, I've reviewed job advertisements for senior pastor vacancies across the United Kingdom on several Christian job websites. Interestingly, only one advert in the last six months actually used the term *senior leader*. Some of the job descriptions and corresponding application forms are extremely detailed. It is evident that each recruitment committee has meticulously sought to thrash out in fine detail what it's hoping for from its new recruit. However, I was left questioning if these committees have truly understood what they need. One job description requested a senior pastor who would agree with the vision and mission of the church and work closely with the leadership team—the committee was actually looking for a team player, who would not rock the boat. Similarly, in another advert, the committee was looking for someone who would take a position on the board of elders. Those committee members wanted someone with a proven track record who would lead their church into a new era of growth and work closely in decision making with both the existing staff team and the small congregation. They wanted a superhero! They wanted a pastor, teacher, evangelist and administrator. The big question then is: who is suited to the job?

The answer is dependent on two things: what does the candidate want, and how do they envision fitting the mold that has been provided? A suitable candidate would be someone who is content to keep the status quo and happily pastor the existing flock; they would be content to work within the confines of the leadership team without rocking the boat and would be satisfied to make small incremental changes only. However, if the candidate had bigger ideas, then both parties are probably asking for trouble!

The Honeymoon Period

When someone takes on an existing church, there is a six-to-eight-month honeymoon period. In this time, the new leader and their congregation are getting to know one another while the recruitment committee is watching to see if its exacting standards are being met. At the same time, if the new pastor has ideas, he or she is looking to hopefully implement them. Everybody appears happy (on the surface, at least).

Honeymoon is followed by the first year of marriage. For some, this becomes a fruitful partnership between the senior pastor, his leadership team, and the congregation. For others, the nightmares gradually begin—the new pastor begins to see and hear rumblings in the leadership about changes he wants to make, and the congregation becomes concerned that these new ideas might scupper their way of doing things. Such rumblings are at first almost invisible and intangibly felt.

A visit from the head office may follow if they have received phone calls expressing concern. Conversations to discuss what the pastor is trying to achieve may begin. The leadership team becomes increasingly uncomfortable as the senior pastor fails to do what they want, and the senior pastor starts to feel undermined. Both parties are asked by the head office to communicate with one another to try to resolve the issues that have arisen.

All of this usually comes to a head after about two years, at which point the senior pastor ether buckles to demands and returns to the status quo or an uneasy truce is reached. In this scenario, the senior pastor then looks for a new position, or the recruiting committee reconvenes on the quiet to look for ways to get rid of the senior pastor.

What happened? Two different groups of people had two different views on the position being offered.

Chapter 3: Should You Lead Someone Else's Church?

Like the swing in the below illustration, what you want is not always what you get.

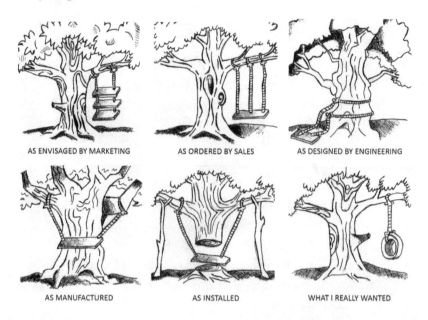

AS ENVISAGED BY MARKETING	AS ORDERED BY SALES	AS DESIGNED BY ENGINEERING
AS MANUFACTURED	AS INSTALLED	WHAT I REALLY WANTED

In the advertisements I mentioned earlier, one problem in particular stood out: the recruiters all wanted someone to fulfill their own expectations of what a pastor should be. They were looking for someone to fulfill their preconceived ideas of what the role of senior pastor should entail. Rarely did an advert clearly state, or even insinuate, that they were searching for a senior leader who could lead and build the church or that they were hoping for someone to bring fresh vision in a new and vibrant way.

To help bring clarity to anyone currently embarking upon a similar recruiting process, here is some help:

Top Tips for Recruiting Boards

1. Do you want a pastor, or do you want a leader? There is a difference! Pastoral work has to do with ministry, - preaching, teaching and adhering to the tenants of the faith, whereas good leadership takes a church forward in its vision, - developing training and raising up young leaders, ensuring finances is growing and looked after and

the implementation of programs that will facilitate growth. The amount of ministry work a senior leader carries out diminishes as the church grows larger. A good senior leader must undertake the role of leadership direction instead. You can have both a pastor and a leader, but when the pastor moves and operates in a leadership mode, the church does and will move forward.

2. If the average age of the congregation is over fifty, don't employ a young pastor in their thirties with a young family— it will kill them! The older the congregation, the more staid the members have become in their ways. Get someone who is semiretired or in their fifties with no aspirations.

3. If you want a younger person, you must give them freedom to grow their own vision in their own way. Let the young pastor see you as sounding boards of wisdom, not as brick walls and voices of disapproval. Give your leader the authority to run the show; don't keep introducing obstacles. As long as there are no emotional or character issues (if there are, then the person should never have been chosen in the first place), you should hand over the spiritual reins of the church.

4. Don't get someone straight out of Bible school. Only rarely has this worked, and then only because the person was extremely mature and sound in doctrine and belief. Normally it would leave a candidate broken and disillusioned.

5. Be willing to step aside once the recruiting process is complete; let the successful applicant grow in the role.

Top Tips for Candidates

1. Find out as much as you can about the church from other sources, not just the information given by the recruiting board.

2. Understand the demographic (population, churches, hospitals, schools) of the local area, and measure these against your own hopes and expectations. Taking on a church of 10 to 15 people in a small village with a population of 350 is unlikely to result in you building a church of 1,500.

3. If there has been a church split previously, speak to people who may know what happened (some would say this isn't a good idea, but you do need to know what you are getting into). I suggest you speak to the denomination head or regional leader and ask very probing questions, while remembering that there are always two sides to a story!

4. Write down all the changes you would like to introduce over the next two years. That way there are no surprises for the board or congregation, who will then know what's coming. Things can always change if you need them to.

5. Ask to look at the finances. If they are not a generous church, you might have an uphill battle to get financial backing for expansion.

6. Negotiate, negotiate, and negotiate! If they want you they will be willing to accept your changes. Alternatively, if you are certain God wants you in that particular area, realize there are other options available (you could always church plant).

I have often wondered what a letter from St Paul to a church recruitment committee would look like I have added one below:

To the Leadership

Fickle Christian Centre.

Fickle-under-Lyme.

Re: Senior leadership Pastor

To whom it may concern,

I would like to apply for the above mentioned position advertised on the Christian Jobs website.

I have many qualifications that I think will impress you. I have been empowered by the Holy Spirit to preach and have had some small success as a writer. Some say I have a gifting as an organiser, I have planted a number of churches but have not stayed very long in any of them. The longest I ever stayed in one place was about three years. I love missions and am a dab hand at organising mission tours. I have been a leader in most places I have served.

However in an endeavour to be frank, open and honest my ministry has not always been appreciated by a great number of people. I am over 50 years of age. Sometimes I have had to leave a town or city because through my powerful preaching I upset a few people.

I have to confess that I do have a criminal record and have served time in jail, but I have always maintained that I was innocent and in most cases I was set up. My health isn't good and I suffer from eye strain, but I can still put in a full days hard work.

Most churches I have been in have been small and I have had to seek other employment in order to meet my needs. Many religious leaders from other churches and denominations do not like my candid way of speaking, they have threatened me, sued me and even attacked me physically. I am not good at keeping records and I do forget people that I have baptised.

I humbly submit the above information and ask that you prayerfully consider my application.

Paul
Apostle appointed by Christ Jesus.

Be honest, would you have given such a person a job to lead your church?

Summary and Advice Checklist

Hopefully the tips above will help people understand that the right person needs to be in the right place at the right time. To those recruiting, remember it's God's church, not yours, and that your views and thoughts may not be his views and thoughts.

Chapter 3: Should You Lead Someone Else's Church?

To those looking to go into ministry, know that taking on someone else's church can either be incredibly rewarding or an absolute nightmare that could maim you for life. However, if you find yourself in that nightmare scenario, you could try the following:

- Meet with your leaders and the board that recruited you. Take someone you trust.

- Renegotiate your plans and bring clarity about where you want to take the church. Ask if they can get on board. Compromise only those things that are not important.

- Negotiation is the key; the more you negotiate, the fewer surprises for both parties.

- If they seem contrary, then negotiate an honorable exit strategy.

- If you still feel strongly that you should be in that town, then consider a future church plant.

- Read Acts 18:7.

- Go to the next chapter to read step four.

4

Should You Plant a Church?

Chapter 4: Should You Plant a Church?

Step Four: Ask Yourself If You Should Plant a Church

A little while ago, I sat in the office of a young man who is not yet thirty but who I believe is destined to be a great leader in the church here in the United Kingdom. We were discussing, among other things, the topic of church planting. It amused me to hear that whereas I used the term *church plant*, he used more contemporary terms, such as *extension service* and *campus*. The principles underpinning his language and my own were the same, and yet across a single generation, the language we each used to describe the expansion of the church had changed. After some thought, I concluded it's not only our language that has changed; so too has the way we establish new churches. The entire culture of church planting has changed.

It is my opinion that we do not have enough churches. We need more, a lot more! I'm not talking about denominations, because we have enough of those (about thirty-three thousand at last count). I'm talking about young, vibrant, contemporary churches. We need churches that are relevant to our communities and to the message of the cross.

Whatever the language we use, beginning new churches is pioneering, but it need not be a step of faith into the unknown. In some cases this has been the domain of a denomination with a dedicated church-planting department (with a small budget).

For others, it has been the desire and domain of only the brave. Historically, church plants have been established from a denominational base. After a short period of time, around twelve months, perhaps, the initial financial support is removed, and the victim, sorry, church planter, is left to their own devices. I admit to being intentionally overly dramatic here to make my point, although I've seen this sink or swim attitude with my own eyes many times. Church planting in the twenty-first century should, I feel, be somewhat different.

Others have covered this subject far better in recent years than I ever could. However, below are a number of things to consider on the matter, both from my own observations and from other people:

Church Planting Should Be at the Heart of the House

In the next chapter, I explain that one of the signs of a healthy church is that it has an outreach program. The desire to reach the lost for Christ is central to the vision of a church that has a desire to plant (or to form extension services, or however one may choose to label it). It is at the core of the church's heart and a strategic element in its growth. There are many examples of large churches all over the world who have had church planting at the heart of their vision.

Don't Run Before You Can Walk

Pioneering a church is hard work—be sure it is what you want to do. There is a physical and spiritual cost to everything, and church planting is no exception.

Think Strategically

Several months ago, I was at a church leader's conference and was given an in-house magazine. In it was an article about a new campus this church was launching in London. It impressed me because these people had clearly done their homework on the city. They had targeted a particular area and knew how many churches already existed within it, as well as the size of each congregation. They knew how many schools were in the area, and how big they were. They looked at restaurants, shopping centers and entertainment centers. This church's leaders were thinking strategically—they were looking at the demographics of their new locality and building a plan accordingly.

There is a reason that Hillsong Church, based in Australia, for example, has chosen capital cities and large metropolises around the world. It is part of their strategy. Even when you study the book of Acts and read about Paul's travels, you see that he had a strategy of where to go and where he wanted to plant churches.

It's Not about Facilities or Finances; It's about People. But …

Church plants often begin with limited finances and resources. Although things may not be perfect, resist the inevitable temptation to focus on the obstacles in front of you. See the opportunities instead! That being said, there are certain practical choices and arrangements you will need to make at the outset. If someone has agreed to support you financially, then clearly a cold and damp village hall may not be a great choice. Consider instead a large hotel conference room with modern facilities and sound proofing. People are attracted to a place where they will feel comfortable and won't have to think about whether their car is safe. Also consider local transport links and whether the facility is easily accessible. If you want people to come, they need to be able to get there! One church I know of planted a church right next to a major transport hub for trains and buses, it resulted in great success.

Start from Strength, not Weakness

There is a cost. Be prepared to send out forty or fifty people from your existing congregation to help populate the new campus or plant. Be prepared to release your best. Church planting experts believe that this number is the minimum required to establish a base and a presence in a community. There is a leadership cost; you will lose some of your best and brightest. The upside of this is that it will release others to take their place where gaps appear. Be prepared also to cover the financial cost required to ensure a solid start. Two to three years should be the norm for this financial help (not twelve months, as is common). It would be massively unhelpful for the planting senior leader to feel panicked and end up having to secure extra income with an additional job.

Don't Transfer Your Problems

It's not a good idea to get rid of difficult people who are causing you problems. If you transfer them from the central hub to the church plant, the problems are merely spread around and not actually dealt with. At the same time, you are giving the leader of the church plant a headache!

Team Building Takes Time

Before you plant, you should ensure that your leadership teams work well together and that they have been together for some time. I know of one church that planted in another European country by sending a number of families out. However, as early as three years prior to this, they sent three of their leaders (and their wives) to intensive language classes. Monthly trips to the European city then ensued, which turned into weekly stays twice each month, and then into six monthly stints, until they were immersed in the new language and culture. This also helped establish a national base.

There Are Bound to Be Disasters!

Not everything will work perfectly; there are bound to be times when things don't mesh. Don't panic! It is all part of the learning process for you and your teams. Remember that while you are instilling a spirit of excellence, you're also building a family, and families aren't perfect. Not very long ago, a pastor said to me that he wanted all his leadership and volunteers to have fun doing church. Be ready to go with the flow, and don't make it boring!

Church Planting Is Not "Sheep Stealing"

You are planting a church to reach the lost, not to deplete another person's field. Too many churches talk about their growth when really it's only growth by influx. People see what you are doing and like it more than the staple diet they are getting at their own church. It is good to discourage this from the beginning so that other local pastors see you are trying to establish something new. The downside to this is that people who have problems and are considered by their own pastors as problem people are attracted to your church, and in the early days of church planting, this can prove to be a distraction from the real work at hand. However, the forty or fifty people who have come with you from the mother church should help to disseminate the heart and culture of the house.

Build Relationships with Other Pastors

Whether you're the one taking the lead or the one sending out a leadership team to plant, it's important to build relationships with other local pastors. Because of your integrity with regard to the previous point, they will hopefully see you as a colleague rather than a threat. Pioneering is a lonely job, and you will need these people. Their prayer support, local knowledge, and experience will be valuable to you at some point. Remember, you are all on the same team. Invite them to your big events, and be prepared to attend theirs from time to time.

Running Home to Mommy Doesn't Always Work

Initially, the relationship with your central hub is very important. Particularly because of the way modern twenty-first-century church planting works, you will always have a strong leadership and relational link. However, there will come a time when you will have to make the decisions and take the lead. The culture and heart of the house will be the same, but the community will be different.

Summary and Advice Checklist

In summary, make church planting part of your outreach vision. Be prepared to lose your best leaders to it, and ensure they have a strong financial and initial membership base. People attract people! Be prepared to plant in the right place at the right time with the right people. In other words, think strategically. Build strong relationships with those around you and others in the community. Above all, remember your mission—it is all about reaching people for the cause of Christ Jesus. Think about the following:

- If you have a heart for church planting, is it part of your present church's vision?

- Never go it alone; always try to build with a team. Paul always had people with him when he planted churches.

- If you plant without financial support from a central hub (unadvisable), you must ensure you have a good job and that your own family is secure.

- Be willing to pay the price.

5

Why Churches Grow

Chapter 5: Why Churches Grow

Step Five: Recognize Why Churches Grow

It is my firm conviction that God's desire is to do things big! I am equally certain that he is supremely able to do things big! I don't think many Christ followers would disagree with me, and yet often I've been asked by leaders of small churches, "Why do I have to be big? Why can't I have a small successful church?" On the face of it, these are two valid questions. However, in my opinion (and experience), they are often an indication of what may be going on under the surface. It may be that the leader is actually unable to make things grow. Perhaps he or she doesn't know how to or has never been taught. This results in obscure statements, such as, "We have quality in our church, not quantity." My retort is usually, "You should have both!"

If your church is 50 strong in a community of 250,000, and you have been in the area for 25 years, then put simply, you're either not doing your job, or you are not the right person for the job. The church is and has always been missional!

In the past decade, I've had the opportunity to observe five large and highly successful churches in New Zealand and Australia. Two of these five churches could be considered mega-churches. The other three have congregations ranging from 120 to 350. These churches are situated in different areas—both large cities and small towns; their common denominator is that they are seeing constant and sustained growth. Having had the opportunity to talk to their senior leaders, It became crystal clear that none of them started out believing that God does small. They believed in a big God who is capable of doing big things. The Internet is full of lists examining the factors that contribute to church growth. I've no doubt these are useful, and many will be more comprehensive than mine. However, they are often written by the senior leader themselves and, as such, have their own bias and slant on the matter. My list is from the perspective of an outside observer.

Vision

The first thing all of these churches had in common was a vision. Without it, they would have had no purpose or direction. Each leader had a clear understanding of what he believed was God's vision for his church, leaders, community, city, and, in some cases, the nation and beyond.

Vision was broken down into two areas: the "here and now" and the "far off." In both I saw a clearly defined way of outworking and accomplishing the vision. The vision for the short term was highly detailed, while the vision for the long term was less so.

For example, the vision statement for one church is "to empower a new generation." Complementing this, the leadership has a clearly defined set of values that lay down the culture of the church and a mission statement to clearly set out *how* it will empower the new generation.

The day-to-day details are thought through and strategically planned—reaching the lost, working in the community, running discipleship programs, and getting the new generation involved in kingdom building. Simultaneously, however, the leadership also looks ahead to the future. The leadership team's members see the influence of their church growing and prepare for their mission field to expand. Thus the outworking of the vision has a "far off" aspect that is reflected in multiple campuses in nearby towns and in programs to impact these communities for Christ.

The Bible says that without vision a nation will perish (Proverbs 29:18 KJV). Often some churches have no clear understanding of, or lack the will to establish, a clearly defined vision. Many leaders believe God will make it happen despite them. While it is true that we must certainly need him to be at the center of it all, it is also true that God left the establishment of the worldwide church to twelve disciples—everyday people!

What are you doing to generate, define, process and pass on the vision God has given you for your church? Remember, small vision will have a small results, so think big!

Leadership

For the church to succeed, church leaders cannot work independently of the vision laid down by the senior leader.

To do so would result in chaos, as in the illustration below.

What about MY Vision?

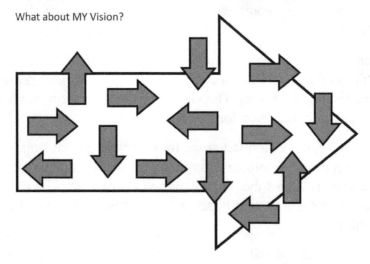

The Bible says, "All we like sheep have gone astray. Each one to his own way" (Isaiah 53:6 KJV). I realize I have taken the Scripture out of context here, but the point I want to make is that all five of the senior leaders I talked to had taken steps to ensure all their leaders were on the same page. Every department of each church has a clear understanding of the central vision and of what their part is in fulfilling that vision. Their roles are clearly defined, and their objectives are in line with the main vision and goals of the church. In this way, individual kingdoms are discouraged, and a single unified church is built, as in this second illustration.

What about OUR Vision?

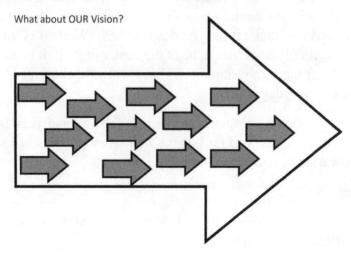

If a leader does not agree with the direction the church is moving (and does not want to or cannot change), the senior leader has the right to ask the leader to step down or find another church where he or she will feel more comfortable.

Time

I visited all five churches on numerous occasions, yet only once did one of them run overtime during a Sunday service. All of them worked to a schedule and made use of a run sheet. Everyone knew what his or her role for that morning was. If the service was advertised as running for ninety minutes, it ran for ninety minutes.

Time is important because it is a limited resource. Every one of the senior leaders recognized the importance and value of people's time. This was evident not only in their conversations with me, but also because they each limited their sermon to twenty-five to thirty minutes, they always started services on time, and they recognized the value of the time given to the church by their volunteers.

When I first arrived in the United Kingdom, I visited a number of churches and was horrified when the preachers often preached for well over an hour. It was as if they felt their congregations had turned up only to listen to them! People's attention spans (especially young people) are rarely more than twenty minutes. Leaders of successful churches recognize this and communicate more effectively for doing so.

Starting on time is a must! It demonstrates your professionalism and that you know what you are about. Too many churches are haphazard in their starting times. Your Sunday morning service is the shop window to who you are. Showing visitors that you can keep to time speaks volumes to them; they will feel that their own time has not been wasted.

Volunteers

All five churches had a large committed group of volunteers. Many gave more than just a few hours each Sunday to serve—they often gave up to three days or evenings. The senior leaders of the five churches I studied recognized the value of the time given by the numerous volunteers. These people were well trained and did everything with a spirit of excellence, like a well-oiled machine. Did these churches and their cohorts of volunteers make mistakes? Of course, but they learned from them to ensure that they were better and more prepared the next time. They were highly committed and did everything with willing hearts and joyful spirits. Often they did this for no immediate reward or recognition. They were continually mindful of the bigger picture when appreciating why they were there—to help win people for Christ. This was reward enough. In all volunteers there comes a point when the result of what they do becomes real and meaningful; this is when they realize that what they do is not a waste of time. It did not matter if the volunteer handled the parking lot, the children's church or was part of the cleaning team, they were reaching the lost for Christ.

The senior leaders sought to recognize the commitment of their volunteers in various ways. Two of the churches had a "person of the week" as part of their announcements on a Sunday morning. Even if that person were on duty that morning, they would be invited to the front of the auditorium and publicly thanked for serving (one church even gave the honored volunteer a bar of chocolate). The leadership would then come forward, lay hands on, and pray for that volunteer. From my observations, this had a twofold effect: it told the volunteer they were appreciated, and it demonstrated to visitors how the church looked after and honored those who served.

All the churches held an end of year dinner for their volunteers, which was paid for by the church (although I know that initially volunteers paid for themselves). At this event, team leaders recognized people for their contributions.

Without a committed core of volunteers, these churches could not have accomplished all that they had. Each of the leaders I spoke to recognized this and spoke incredibly highly of their volunteer workforce.

Outreach

A church cannot accomplish what Jesus has called us to accomplish if it is not reaching the lost for Christ. It is alarming that many small churches of fifty or so people have little or no outreach program. All of the senior leaders from the five churches being studied said that from the very beginning they had outreach programs to reach the lost. The bigger they have grown, the more prominent these programs have become. Examples include: small evangelistic outreaches, Alpha courses, food banks, night shelters for the homeless, preschools, mother and tots days, holiday programs for kids, and much, much more. The church can do far much more than government agencies in reaching people and showing them they have value and worth!

When a businessman starts a business, he tries various things until he finds what works. Similarly, not all the programs and courses introduced in these churches worked. They were canned for other more successful programs. The focus remains on the calling and vocation to reach out to a lost and broken world with the message of the cross, and on the answer to this world's problems—Jesus.

Summary and Advice Checklist

These churches were successful because they have in common the five things I observed and detailed above. All the churches had been operating for between five years to twenty-five years, and all were seeing rapid growth (and have continued to do so). There is hope for your church if you have been stuck at a congregation size of forty to fifty. I believe fervently that a church leader can build a large, vibrant, healthy, and contemporary church with God's help and intervention. As long as they are willing to learn and make the sacrifices required to grow a congregation, growth is possible.

If you are a senior leader, reflect on the following:

- Do you have a clear vision and plan for your church?

- Is the vision agreed on and supported by all your leadership?

- Do you support, train, and encourage volunteers?

- Remember, time is important to people. Value and respect this, and they will do the same for you.

- Value the commitment that volunteers give.

- Sit down and strategically plan some outreach programs with the sole aim of reaching the lost. Think outside the normal church box—movie nights at church don't always cut it!

- It isn't about the fact you may have a small church, it is about reaching the lost for Christ. If you are doing that, then in my eyes, you are not a small church.

- Read on to the next chapter and reflect on step six.

6

Why Churches Don't Grow

Step Six: Recognize Why Some Churches Don't Grow

In the last chapter, I gave five observations or habits that make churches grow. In this chapter I will explore twelve reasons why I believe some churches do not grow. I must reiterate that these are merely my observations. They aren't based on statistics or data I have collected. They are based on real situations from my own experiences of helping failing churches turn their situations around.

A Lack of Clear Vision and Implementation

If vision is a cause for success, then it stands to reason that lack of vision is a cause for failure. If a church doesn't know where it's going, it will never get to where the senior leader wants it to go. It isn't enough for the senior leader to merely present a vision to the members of his congregation (although it's a good start). He also needs to communicate how he will implement, progress, and evaluate it. A number of years ago, when I was learning how to scuba dive, my instructor told us we had to learn to "plan the dive and then to dive the plan." In other words, we had to plan everything and stick to that plan. At a basic level, a church vision is a plan of where we see our churches in any given period. For example, if we want to see our church grow from forty to fifty people in a twelve-month period, vision sees the fifty and then implements a plan to reach and attain that goal. It sticks to the plan (perhaps making only minor changes). The larger a church grows and the more extensive the fulfilling of a vision is, the more complex the implementation may be. It's good to have a big vision, but it is important to take baby steps toward it, with clearly defined goals. The more baby steps that are accomplished, the more confident the church will become. With confidence rising, more daring plans and steps can be taken.

Trying to Please Everyone All the Time

Pastors often fail in churches because they try very hard to please everyone—they don't want to lose people. There is not an organization anywhere on earth that can please everyone all the time! I am often amused by people who vote for an electoral candidate and then get upset when this same candidate votes with his or her party on an issue they are personally against. They fail to understand that their vote was not just for a single candidate but for a political party who must govern and do what the party, as a whole, believes is right for the nation.

In the same way, senior leaders of churches cannot expect to please everyone. Some decisions will upset people, but if you're sure that it will take the church where God wants it to be, you must be decisive. Convince people of the rightness of what you are proposing. It's important that the culture and values of the church have been and are being clearly taught; then you can move forward. It's also worth mentioning that there should always be areas you consider nonnegotiable. These are decisions you make from the very beginning and are not prepared to compromise on.

Passionless Leadership

It is often relatively easy for a leader who is pioneering a new church to raise up leaders who are passionate about the vision, culture, and ethos of the church. Those around him have probably been involved in shaping these things and can therefore quite naturally get on board with the direction being taken. However, it may be significantly more difficult for new leaders of established churches to inspire and enthuse established ministry leaders who have already been running their departments for long periods of time. Each area of church life needs people who are passionate about that area to be in charge. For example, you cannot have people who dislike children running kids programs. Maybe they're there because they are skilled in related areas (such as administration), but it simply won't work! In this scenario, you would quickly see young families leave the church to go elsewhere. You must find someone who is passionate to do great things for God in the children's department to lead the children's department. You must train this person; you should spend time instilling your vision and passion into them. Do not be afraid of repositioning or asking people to step aside.

The worst that could happen is that your original Sunday school department head could leave.

Passionless leaders sap the energy out of churches; don't let it happen!

Chapter 6: Why Churches Don't Grow

Dead Ducks

The only nice duck is a roasted one with orange or plum sauce! Alarmingly, however, there are struggling churches everywhere with dead or lame ducks plodding around and wasting effort, time and resources. Clearly, they should have been consigned to the rubbish bin long ago. What are they? They are programs that never worked or are now outdated. The people involved in them are merely going through the motions. This might be your home groups, which have perhaps followed the same format for decades and need to be rethought. Or perhaps your church service is no longer relevant to the younger generation. I remember a proverb or saying doing the rounds in Christian circles in the early 1980s: "The seven words of a dying church—'We've never done it this way before.'" The same applies today. If the program is not working, get rid of it before too much damage is caused.

A Lack of Spiritual Enthusiasm

Some of the churches I go into are like funeral homes (without the dead bodies!). The leaders don't seem to be happy at all. They do not have the faith that God is in control; nor do they seem to believe that prayer can move mountains. Such leaders are often less than enthusiastic about their service. They fail to grasp the truth that their service is actually for Christ, rather than for the church or their fellow leaders.

No wonder people leave such churches! Who would want to stay in a church with a leader who struggles to believe in the God and Scriptures they preach about?

Leaders must be excited about the Bible and about meeting to pray; they should be passionate about their relationship with God and His church. This enthusiasm needs to be transmitted via the pulpit, the office, the home group, and in private at every opportunity.

Risk Aversion

Risk taking is a must for any church seriously hoping to reach a broken world. Steps of faith must be taken, not only by the leadership but also by the entire congregation. Failing churches have often lost sight of their Hebrews 11:1 "moment"—the certainty of things unseen. They haven't given their people an opportunity to see a great God at work. Risk has been replaced by comfort, and the potential for something unbelievable to take place has been overshadowed by certainty.

Lack of Outreach

The lack of an outreach program is probably the most common issue I find among failing churches. Too many churches have become "fellowships" where Christians come together for comfort and good gossip. Church is not, in my opinion, a place for the Christian, but a place for the non-Christian to be brought by the Christian. It is not an exclusive club. Churches like this are doomed to die because they have completely disobeyed the Scriptures. God makes it clear that we are to go everywhere in the world and make disciples (followers of Christ) of all humankind (Matthew 28:19 KJV).

Selfishness

Churches fail because leaders and their congregations have become selfish. They have forgotten that they too were once broken, unloved, and far from God. They have forgotten to see the world through God's eyes.

Uninspiring Worship Services

I grew up in a rather conservative country where the church services revolved around a little red book called *The Redemption Hymnal*. It had for its time some very inspiring hymns, but thank goodness we don't sing them anymore! They no longer have any relevance to today's generation, and frankly, if I came across the book I would burn it before any worship leader got their hands on it! Radical I know. We who are Christians have no need for old music, we should be making new hymns and new music. New music is vital if we are to succeed in attracting this present generation to the church. Our worship services are the church's shop window to attract today's generation. The music style has to inspire and uplift people. The service itself should be interactive, engaging, humming with vibrancy, and full of life.

Chapter 6: Why Churches Don't Grow

A Lack of Functional Structures

All great churches need structure. Structures need to function and interlink with one another. Structure fails when, for example, the newly converted see no formal way to progress in their walk with Christ. When it comes to structure, everyone must be on the same page. They must go through the same processes and move in the same direction. There needs to be cohesion.

A Dead Midweek

A church is not just a Sunday ritual of one or two meetings; rather, it is a whole week of events and meetings: leaders meetings, training, youth meetings, mother and toddler groups, men's breakfasts, and ladies' mornings (to name but a few). Perhaps the most important is a midweek meeting where new people can be nurtured and disciplined into the life and culture of the church. The home group should exude life and direction and purpose. If these meetings are boring and irrelevant, attendance figures will struggle. Every senior leader should endeavor to see at least eighty-five percent of their church involved in midweek home group. Do something about them or die.

The Lack of Friendliness

"We are always there for people" is something I hear often from pastors and leaders, but when I visit their churches I sometimes feel like a wallflower. People don't come talk to me because they are enclosed in their own little holy huddles. This lack of friendliness (and common decency) will be the death of a church very quickly. People are attracted to life and to human contact. If you understand them, you will win them; if you ignore them, you will lose them.

Summary and Advice Checklist

I hope these last two chapters have helped you understand two things: You can succeed in growing a great church for the kingdom of God.

However, without a willingness to change some things, your church is at risk of quickly dying and becoming lost in obscurity.

Consider the following:

- Do you have old traditions in your church that might be holding you back?

- Seek out (or raise up) people of passion, and find creative ways to use them.

- Shoot all dead ducks! Convince people of the need for new and modern programs.

- Believe, teach, and preach that God can and will do great things. Speak it out in all aspects of the church.

- Build functional structures in the church with clear lines of authority and responsibility.

- Encourage people to have fun doing church and to reflect it on their faces (especially when visitors come)!

7

**Establishing Influence and
Stepping Out in Vision**

Chapter 7: Establishing Influence and Stepping Out in Vision

Step Seven: Establish Influence and Step Out in Vision

I speak a lot about vision. For me, it is the starting point of everything we do. Without a clearly defined vision, we are directionless. Vision defines who and what we do, and it defines how we do what we do. Vision sets the agenda for the future direction of the church.

I've said it before, but I am utterly convinced that ministry builds people while leadership builds churches. I believe that a church can grow to only between 120 and 150 people on the ministry of a single person. However, with a firm grasp of leadership and how it functions, that same person can grow their church to way beyond this number. Church is not just about the ability to pastor; it is about influencing people to join your cause, beliefs, and culture. It is the engaging and building of relationships. It is the creation of organization and structure. Big business does not concentrate on the vision; it concentrates on how to manifest that vision through establishing its influence in the market place.

I was once asked to run a leadership seminar for a small church. The pastor had been there for over twenty years. In that time he had seen his church grow to about two hundred, although the congregation had since declined to fewer than fifty members. The pastor told me about the great conferences they had organized for the church movement they were aligned with. He explained that, over the last ten years, great people had come to these conferences and prophesied that God was going to make their church a place of healing and worship and that they would reach out to the surrounding cities. He told me proudly of the various committees he sat on and the local interdenominational council that he chaired.

A few hours prior to the seminar starting, I walked around the surrounding streets to knock on a few doors. Clipboard in hand, I explained to the householders I was conducting a survey and asked if they would mind answering a few questions. I asked them if they knew when the church across the street was established. Were they aware of the outreach and community programs the church ran? Had they ever been to the church? Did they know what the church was called? Did they know the pastor's name? Had the church ever influenced their lives? To my shock and horror, even though the church had been there since 1922, very few people knew anything about the church at all.

Over lunch that day, I shared my findings with the pastor. He told me confidently that the church had indeed been very influential, in the past, which continued to stand them in good stead.

A great many church movements have come and gone. Those which are no more had, over time, deceived themselves into believing the influence they held in the past was sufficient to propel them into their future. It's dumb to think that people will remember a church's achievements. People move on, and so should we! Reinhold Bonnke once said, "Sometimes we sit and wait for God to move, when in fact God is sitting and waiting for you to move." God has already told us what to do—*Go!* Don't sit and expect things to happen. Things happen when we move and when we go. The pastor and his leadership team did absolutely nothing to bring about the prophetic words spoken over them. Instead, they sat back and waited ... and waited. If forward momentum is to be sustained, the establishment of influence, vision, and the dissemination of that vision must be a continual process.

I'm not saying there is a magic formula that when followed will result in massive and spontaneous growth. It is God, and him alone, who sets up increase in the church. That being said, our actions can either hinder or facilitate this increase. It's good to remember that a strong culture, hard work, solid organization, and firm structure will all help produce an atmosphere to encourage growth. Existing congregation members will embrace the vision and the direction they are being taken. When they see God at work, they will be encouraged to become more involved.

So how does a senior church leader step out in vision? We have discussed many other things that are essential for vision, but its implementation and dissemination that need to be looked at in a little more detail.

First, a senior leader should train their mind to think and see possibilities rather than barriers and problems. They need an attitude of optimism and faith. Their vision should be unique—adopting the vision of a favorite mega-church brings only short-term results and equally a short lifespan. Such a vision is not birthed in the heart, but rather in the visual and in the knowledge of what someone else has achieved. Instead, the vision should be based on prayer and time spent in God's Word.

Once the vision is set, they must discuss it at every opportunity, with colleagues, leaders and their own team. The leadership team of a church should be speaking about it frequently, and everything the team does should be directed back to the vision and direction of the church. Leaders assume responsibility for the vision and seek to drive it forward. This involves taking responsibility for both success and failure. Not everything tried will work.

A word of caution: if a leader is distracted by and stops at every failure, they are no longer leading but merely reacting to events. A leader in this position has reverted to the comfort of operating from a ministry stance, rather than a leadership position, they revert to just their preaching and teaching rather than sticking to the strategic plan. In other words, they have "bottled it." Strong leaders resist this urge to return to old ways.

A senior leader works hard, sometimes up to sixty hours a week or more. They invest time, energy, and money in the vision. Others should be encouraged to do the same, and as the church grows, they in turn may release others to more substantial roles in the church. Potential leaders can and should be identified early and then motivated, trained, and released to make the vision a reality. The ministry load can then be shared with no reservations.

It's important that the senior leader seeks to grow constantly in both spiritual and personal development. Constant growth allows for capacity increase and, significantly, brings the leader greater confidence, which increases the leader's capacity to lead a church larger than his current one.

Foresight in expounding vision is vital. Great leaders can see the outcome of any given scenario, which helps them develop, adapt, and be flexible in what they do and say. That EQ thing again.

Finally, I shall revisit the ministry versus leadership debate. When a person begins (or takes on) a church, he is usually involved in substantial ministry work. However, as the church grows, this person's time should be increasingly spent developing leadership, structuring the establishment, and building culture. Problems arise when a person thinks that because he is employed in a spiritual occupation, his time should be fully committed to ministry.

The graph below, which I have adapted from Dr. Ian Jagelman of the Jagelman Institute of Australia, ((used with his permission) better represents the percentage of time spent between ministry and leadership.

When the congregation size of a church is between fifty and sixty-five people, a pastor spends about 90 percent of their time on ministry matters and 10 percent on leadership matters.

At around 135 people, he spends equal amounts of time on each. From then on, the senior leader becomes more involved with leadership decisions and less involved in ministry.

Once a church gets to 500 or more members, the senior leader spends 90 percent of his or her time on leadership direction and only 10 percent on ministry. Generally speaking, this last 10 percent is preaching.

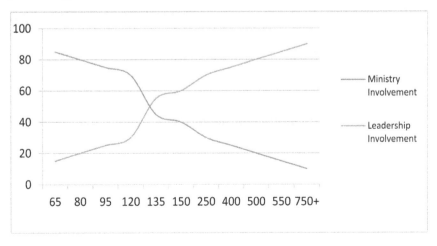

Chapter 7: Establishing Influence and Stepping Out in Vision

Summary and Advice Checklist

The dissemination and implementation of a leader's vision is to fulfill one thing only: the making of disciples and the winning of the lost for the cause of Christ.

Consider the following:

- Your vision may be simple, such as to serve and bring all to Christ. However, don't just say it; disseminate it.

- Live the vision.

- Have a clear idea of how to fulfill the vision.

- Constantly be on the lookout for other leaders who reflect and own the vision.

- A spiritual application always requires a leadership outcome. Ask the question, "If I lead someone to Christ, is there a structure in place to nourish and grow this person to maturity?"

8

The Leader Sets the Culture

Chapter 8: The Leader Sets the Culture

Step Eight: Remember That the Leader Sets the Culture

Whether we like it or not, the senior leader is the one who should be tasked with setting the cultural tone of the church. Culture is the extension of the senior leader's philosophy on how to make the vision of the church a reality; it is the atmosphere in which everything happens. Culture includes the ideas, customs, behaviors, and characteristics of any given group of people. For example, many mega churches around the world have a specific way of modeling how they present and "do" church; this is their culture.

I've said before that I have a holistic view of leadership. The culture of the church is set by the senior leader in all aspects of their lives. Therefore, I firmly believe (as Scripture teaches) that a leader should have a stable home life (1 Timothy 3:4–5). If the leader is married, they should have a supportive spouse and family. I also believe the leader should stay fit through regular exercise and eating a balanced diet. Even these practical areas of life are opportunities for a leader to exert a positive influence on those following. It is also vital (and could perhaps go without saying) for the senior leader to model a fresh and vibrant spiritual life.

A few months ago, I was at a leadership seminar and had the opportunity to discuss this very point with one of the key speakers. He told the following story:

Steve had been asked to take over a church which twenty years earlier he had planted. The church now had a congregation of about 450. At his first Sunday morning service, the place was packed full. Everyone was keen to see the new man in charge. During a lull in the praise and worship, a man some rows behind the leader bellowed out a prophetic word (these things are not unexpected in Pentecostal churches). The following week, Steve stood up to give the notices, and while doing so he pointed to a new form. He politely instructed the congregation to write their praise reports or prayer requests on it, and explained that the forms would be read out by the leadership each week for everyone in the congregation to rejoice in or pray for.

Also, if anyone should have a prophetic word, they too should write it on the aforementioned form and submit it to the leadership before the service. Steve's approach provided the church leadership the opportunity to determine whether or not the prophecy was in keeping with what they felt the Holy Spirit was saying to the church. With this simple system, Steve made sure that the leaders, not the congregation member, were in control of setting the culture of the church. It was his conviction that the Sunday morning service is the shop window of his church, and he wanted any visitors in attendance to feel comfortable. The leadership, and not the prophet, would judge if the prophetic word was in keeping with the moving of the Holy Spirit. This, he felt, was in keeping with the New Testament teaching.

The result of this cultural readjustment was that over two hundred people left the congregation during his first twelve months in charge. They mistakenly believed that Steve was against prophecy! Nothing could be further from the case; it was his conviction that there were more appropriate and helpful opportunities in church life where it should take place. Over the following 18 months, more than 250 people joined the church.

What Defines Church Culture?

The Right Words

The way we speak will be reflected by those around us. If we are always optimistic, those around us will usually be optimistic. If we exude faith, so will those who follow us. If we are super spiritual and religious, those around us will be just the same. People who don't understand us will leave; It is more likely those we reach will be more like ourselves.

Several years ago, I took my daughters along to an Easter service at a classical Pentecostal church. When we entered, I felt as though I had transported back in time to my teenage years. Afterward, the friendly pastor asked me if I was washed in the blood of the Lamb. I understood perfectly what he was saying, but my daughters did not. I had to explain to them what he meant. No one was going to be bathing in lambs blood, nor were there any people ready to pour blood all over them, they were safe. No wonder his congregation was small, ineffective, and full of geriatrics. His intentions were good, but his words and language were inappropriate and outdated. Today's generation of young believers know what it is to be a Christian, but they don't use phrases such as "being born again" or "washed in the blood of the Lamb." If we want to reach this generation, we need to get the culture of church language right. We need to learn to use words they easily understand. I am not meaning that we should dumb things down, sin is sin, rather that we be aware of the religious jargon we use with strangers.

The Philosophy of Ministry

We all hold tightly to a set of deeply held beliefs through which we individually determine a basic understanding of life. Such beliefs are usually held at a subconscious level and are incredibly powerful, often most evident when we switch to our "default settings" in stressful situations. They are shaped by the way we were raised, our education, the information we gather, religious and spiritual input, relationships, and general life experience. A senior leader will discover that these beliefs are reflected strongly in their approach to ministry. It is important that they remain aware of this reality, because from time to time a leader will need to work hard to deviate from their default settings in order to make the right call for a particular situation.

A leader is also required to be aware of, and seek to change when necessary, the default settings of other people. Changing someone's belief system is rarely achieved by doing a course or going to a conference, which do not fundamentally change what a person believes. Rather, if such change is to be effected, an individual needs constant input and reinforcement from someone they respect and trust. It could take many forms: leadership training, setting an example, vision casting, and the sharing of success stories are just a few suggestions. People need to hear a new idea and then see it being successfully implemented to be convinced. Given plenty of time, people can learn to adopt different ways of thinking

The Nonnegotiable

This was briefly mentioned earlier. Senior leaders should determine things they are not willing to negotiate on.

These ideas or values should be expressed in the core values of the church to be transmitted from the leadership team outward. Senior leaders should not be indecisive, pessimistic, and boring. These are not the values you want to see in a growing, vibrant culture.

Traditions

Even the most successful, contemporary, and vibrant churches have traditions. These are not always bad; however, you should be prepared to question them and their viability. Are there things in our churches that are there by default but are not conducive to church growth? I was in one church that regularly held an evening where the congregation members were openly invited to share whatever they felt was on their hearts either in speech or song. When I asked the senior pastor why they held this event, he told me it was because they always had done so. In other words, it was a tradition. I could see that the evening did not have any great success and was based on one Scripture, 1 Corinthians 14:26.

After attending several of these meetings, I realized that they also brought division and chaos. For this church, there was no viable reason for continuing with a meeting of this kind. It was purely tradition; it was a dead duck! I pray that God would help us address those things that are preventing us from growing and give us wisdom, courage, and grace to make changes.

Measurement

We all like to measure success, and how we measure it both reveals and reinforces our culture. It's important that we measure the right things in the right way if we are to gain a real understanding of our success or failure. For example, we might count the number of people attending a Sunday service but neglect to track the number of people who are giving their lives to Christ. Furthermore, we should be measuring growth in other programs within the church to see if the increase in new converts is being reflected. Core programs, such as small groups, baptismal classes, and discipleship courses, should also be growing. Otherwise, how can we claim to be fulfilling the mission of the church to reach out and make disciples of people?

Chapter 8: The Leader Sets the Culture

We must define what success looks like for us, and this can be a very revealing question.

Do we truly want to see new converts being made disciples of Christ and in turn bringing their own "worlds" to know Christ, or is our primary driver to have the biggest Sunday congregation in the area so that we look and feel successful?

Fashions and Behavior

Culture follows fashion and behavior, not the other way around. It's currently fashionable in the church to use a Bible app on an iPhone rather than a paper Bible. A more traditional church may want to reflect its traditions or its pious behavior. In both examples, these things have become our cultural norms. Now, it may sound silly, but few senior leaders I know could retain young people in their churches because of their personalities alone. If they suddenly insisted that all the women wear hats on Sunday morning, for example, they would lose their youth in droves. Senior church leaders must be relevant to today's society. We cannot expect to have growing, vibrant, contemporary churches if we insist on following the norms of a bygone age. If I have to wear skinny jeans and learn all about the latest technology to help me reach the next generation, I will do so. It's about doing real life together, not conforming to the religious overtones of my grandfather.

Summary and Advice Checklist

Senior leaders need to be intentional about creating culture from the planning level. Culture must be prepared for and deliberately reflected in everything we do. If we fail to create the right culture, we risk ending up as paranoid, narcissistic, people pleasing, God-dishonoring leaders. Take the following advice to help develop the right culture in your church:

- Don't use obsolete and old-fashioned language. Young people enjoy it when the senior leader tries to be hip and modern. The emphasis here is on the word tries. Ensure that all your leaders do the same.

- If your culture is to make church fun, then have fun! But never let fun detract from the message.

- Appoint someone to lead your services (an MC) who is a cultural ambassador. This person must embody the culture and take every opportunity to naturally communicate it from the platform.

- Look around and get rid of any tired traditions that are no longer relevant.

- Measure everything. For example, measure attendance at all meetings, not just the Sunday services. This gives an indication how people are becoming involved in the various areas of the church. Measure how many people go to home groups, how much is given financially and when, and so on.

- Learn about and use the latest technology.

- Listen to your children (and grandchildren).

- Talk about the culture of the church often.

- Make sure church culture is clearly defined and easily explainable.

9

Strategic Planning

Step Nine: Engage in Strategic Planning

I am amazed by the number of church leaders I meet who don't know how to strategically plan. Sadly, strategic planning is not something normally taught at Bible college or seminary. A few church leaders can tell me what they want for their churches right now, and some can tell me their plan for the next twelve months. However, most leaders I've met do not know where they want their church to be in three to five years' time, and even fewer would have a plan for the next ten years. "God will take care of that," they often say to me.

Reinhardt Bonnke once said, "Sometimes we sit and wait for God to move, when in fact God is waiting for us to move." There are some church leaders who excuse their lack of success by insisting that they are waiting for God to move. The problem with this thinking is that when God does move, they don't have the experience or wherewithal to sustain the growth and retain the converts that result from this sudden move of God.

Other leaders try to plan, but they don't understand the concept or the detail required. They may find that they do not have the training or organizational skills to maintain a healthy, large church. They use a "pay-as-you-go" type of leadership.

Then there are leaders who realize they don't have the abilities to raise up the other leaders required to sustain growth and continue the increase. This inadequacy can often lead to paranoid leadership because when new leaders finally do emerge to fill the obvious gaps, the original band of leaders becomes suspicious.

So what is strategic planning as it relates directly to our churches?

Simply put, strategic planning is an attempt to position the church within its environment. It is fully understanding where we have come from and how we got here, and then knowing where we want to go and how we want to get there. Before an organization or movement can form a strategic plan, it needs to have already done four things:

- Defined a clear vision (where they are going).

- Identified their core values. These values underpin who they are at a foundational level. They shape practices, decisions, and thought processes. Such values are nonnegotiable.

- Set out a clear process by which the vision can be accomplished.

- Write it down and chart the course of actions to be taken.

Both Jesus and the early church planned strategically. I cannot think of a better argument than this to support my conviction that we must do the same, so let's investigate the claim more thoroughly. It almost goes without saying that I cannot possibly go into great detail on such an intensive and exciting subject; the subject could be a complete book by itself! Nevertheless, I will explore three key questions:

Did Jesus and the Early Church (as We Read in Acts) Have a Vision?

If I had to put Christ's vision for the world into today's language, I would say his vision is "to reach out to a lost and broken world and to restore its relationship with its creator."

God put into motion his plan for redemption at the very moment the world first sinned. His plan would result in his son reaching out and sacrificing his life so that a lost and broken world could once again have a restored relationship with, and through, their creator.

The early church also had a vision—to fulfill what Jesus told them to do to: "Go into the whole world and make disciples of all mankind" (Matthew 28:19). We can see throughout the book of Acts that this was certainly the vision followed by the early church.

Which Values Were Not Negotiable to Jesus and the Early Church?

These values are clearly expounded in Matthew 5–7 (the Sermon on the Mount), where Jesus taught his disciples about belief and practice:

1. Let your life be a demonstration of who you are and what you believe. Jesus always stayed true to who he was and to his purpose. The members of the Acts church believed in

what they were doing because they had a mandate from the Messiah to do it.

2. Get your priorities right. Put God first in all you say and do.

3. Make sure your heart and life reflect what you believe and practice.

4. Avoid sexual sin.

5. Be careful with your words, and let your yes be yes and your no, be no. If you are decisive and honest with people, they will trust and respect you.

6. Listen well and take that extra bit of time with people.

7. Be generous with everything you have, remembering your reward is not in this world. Make money work for you; don't become a slave to money.

8. Grow spiritually, in prayer and fasting, and in the Word. These things build the spirit and bring us closer to God.

9. Continue to do what you are asked to do, and know that God will provide all your needs. When your priorities are in order, God will meet you exactly where you are.

10. Other people are just as important as you. Treat people in the same way as you would want to be treated. Learn to see people in the same way that God sees them.

11. Persevere, knowing that things will get tough but that God will always come through for you.

12. Stay away from things that could lead you astray. Stay focused on God.

13. Do everything from a pure motive. We reap what we have sown. If we put good things into others, we will receive a great return.

14. When doing life with people, always use the right building materials, and build in the right place. Be in God's purpose and God's plan.

So Did Jesus and the Early Church Have an Action Plan?

How did Jesus, in bodily form, plan to put the vision into action? Luke 4:18–30 describes one occasion when Jesus made his plan of action extremely clear. His instructions were to preach the good news, proclaim freedom, heal the blind, release the oppressed, and take the message to the whole world. We see throughout Jesus' ministry that he did all of these time and time again. He did exactly what he said he would do. Jesus even went out of the borders of his own country to strategically plant seed: he went north to the Syro-Phoenician woman, he went east to the Gaderean and the demon-possessed man, and he went to Samaria to the woman at the well.

It stands to reason that Luke (who also recorded the events of Jesus' life) would be likely to demonstrate how the early church followed Jesus' action plan even after his ascension. Indeed, the book of Acts records for us that on the day of Pentecost, the apostle Peter preached, and thousands were saved. Later, we see blind and lame people healed and those bound by demons set free. Both literal and spiritual prisoners are released. It is evident that with the help of the Holy Spirit, the early church did exactly what Jesus told them to do: they took the message of the good news throughout Judea from its central base in Jerusalem.

In the book of Acts we also see Paul, who was sent out after his conversion and a short period of reflection. Over the next two decades, he strategically planned all the towns and cities he would visit. These were not random events but planned visits along major trade routes and population centers.

Now we have seen from Scripture itself that both Jesus and the early church had a strategic plan, which they executed to great effect. I am intensely frustrated and weary of seeing small churches struggling in a spiral of irrelevance. If Jesus is the starting point, we should be starting at the same point he did—with a strategic plan. I am passionate about the church. We are Christ's representatives here in this sinful world. We arc God's "plan A," initiated through the sacrifice of His son Jesus. It is our responsibility to build His church.

Chapter 9: Strategic Planning

I am also passionate about seeing pastors and church leaders get it right. It's absolutely vital every church has a vision in order to move forward. Also, creating a well-defined set of nonnegotiable values is critical. From this point, a church can form a plan of how it will achieve and extend the vision—both in the short term and the long term. Strategic planning is vital and necessary in the church.

How to Write a Strategic Plan

- Start by writing down your vision of where you would like the church to be in a given period of time (two, then five, and then ten years). Sometimes just a sentence or two will be enough.

- Values are important because they will help you shape how you word your mission statement.

- Write down a mission statement. A mission statement is to summarize the church's underlying purpose, or vision. A strategic plan is the extension of your mission statement, which guides the goal-setting process and serves as a means to be able to measure the church's success.

- Set attainable goals (smaller steps along the way) to make things achievable.

- Honestly examine what you, the leader, personally need to accomplish the plan and what you need to put in place to make sure you achieve your goals.

- Look at what you may need from outside the church to help you accomplish your goals.

- Develop a plan that has clearly defined goals of where you want to be in six months, eighteen months, and three years in order to make your big vision a reality.

- Run with the plan!

- After a period of time, create a SWOT analysis (strengths, weaknesses, opportunities, and threats).

- Revisit the plan every six months to make changes where needed.

- Always link the plan to the vision and culture of the church.

- The outcome should always be people.

10

Communication

Chapter 10: Communication

Step Ten: Improve Communication

I sometimes hate the word *communication*. Unfortunately, not everybody knows how you work or operate, hence the need to communicate accurately and succinctly. Communication has just as much to do with understanding the perception of the listener as it has to do with taking care when speaking. People don't just listen to what we say; they respond to how we feel about them. Someone once said, "I think; I say; he hears; he thinks." The secret of communication, therefore, is to get the other to hear and then to think what you think.

If you read the wartime speeches of Winston Churchill, it is evident that he expressed with his words the feelings of the British people. He chose words because they epitomized the view the public held concerning Adolf Hitler. He spoke to his listeners' minds but also to who they were—the unconquerable British people!

I am, in my opinion, a great communicator. However, my wife thinks differently! Sometimes we will discuss a point for hours and eventually reach the conclusion that we both agreed on the same point from the beginning. Something somewhere was lost in translation. The other thing I have noticed is that the older I get, I tend to think a lot about issues and hold the conversation with my wife in my mind. She gets very irritated when I then tell her I have spoken to her about the issue when clearly I have not. Often this has nothing to do with age but more to do with stress and pressure of work.

Church leaders have a similar issue—they think they are communicating their point clearly but in reality the result is often not what they wanted. They get upset because a program or ministry is not moving in the right direction. They blame others, but the problem may have been of their own making.

Recently I did a church audit for a rapidly growing and dynamic church. I interviewed each leader in the church, from the senior pastor to the home group leaders. I asked them, "What is the vision of the church?" To my surprise, after being assured by the senior leader that everybody would know it,

40 percent of the leaders got it wrong! In those cases, they didn't get all the wording wrong, but the emphasis was different from what the senior leader wanted. Their perception of how the vision was being manifested differed from the perception of the senior leadership. Fortunately, in this case, the situation was easily rectified, but that isn't always the case. Communication is something we all need to work on, and thankfully there are many things we can easily and quickly implement to help us do so. Read my tips below for some of these.

Summary and Advice Checklist

1. *Stop talking.* You cannot listen and understand fully if you are doing all the talking.

2. *Put the talker at ease.* Help people feel relaxed in your presence. Not everybody is comfortable speaking to a senior leader.

3. *Show the person you want to listen.* Look and act interested; don't keep looking at your watch or your mobile phone.

4. *Remove distractions.* Close your door, clear your desk (unless you have to take notes), and don't doodle.

5. *Empathize with the other person.* Try to put yourself in the other person's place to understand where he or she is coming from.

6. *Be patient.* Don't start walking to the door! That gives the impression that you would rather be somewhere else.

7. *Hold your temper.* If it's a contentious issue, don't suddenly display anger. An angry person does not communicate or listen accurately.

8. *Go easy on argument and criticism.* People become defensive when we criticize. Even if we win the argument, we might lose the person. Whatever you do, never say, "I am saying this in love" or "You must understand that we here at the church love you, but I feel you are wrong." These statements

say the exact opposite. The other person will not feel loved or understood at all!

9. *Ask questions.* The more questions you ask, the more the other person will feel you are listening. Encourage him or her to develop points further.

10. *Ask for feedback.* Ask someone you can trust if you are a good communicator. Ask also where you can improve.

11. *Try reflective listening.* When you are looking for a specific outcome, ask the listener to repeat what you've said and to explain how he or she is going to do what you asked. Give the listener the freedom to work things out, but do all you can to ensure you both understand each other before moving on.

12. Remember to talk issues through with your wife or husband.

11

Delegation and Decision Making

Chapter 11: Delegation and Decision Making

Step Eleven: Improve Your Delegation and Decision-Making Skills

In this chapter, I would like to give some insight into two areas that can be the making or the breaking of a church—delegation and decision making. Poor attitudes in these areas are responsible for the lack of growth and the ineffectiveness of countless churches throughout the world.

Delegation

Every leader in a growing church will have no doubt seen the need to delegate the responsibilities of their increasing workload. They probably also know delegation isn't an easy task. There are several obstacles to overcome. For example, a leader might resist delegating out of a feeling that they can get the job done to a higher standard, or more quickly, by doing it alone. Conversely, they may feel insecure that the new leader might do a better job and expose weaknesses on their part. There could be concern that the new responsibilities will be too much for the subordinate to handle or that there isn't the necessary time to "hand over" things thoroughly—training and releasing people takes time and effort! It could even be that the leader is anxious to show the congregation that they are "earning their keep." Thankfully, all of these excuses are easily overcome!

A major problem in Christian organizations is that one person makes all the decisions—the senior pastor. As the church grows, the senior pastor continues to make all the decisions. If the church stops growing, the senior pastor is still making all the decisions! Problems occur as the senior pastor loses touch with what is happening as the church grows and in society and in the local community that surrounds the church. This happens when there is a failure to inject dynamic new blood into the vision. Because they have failed to delegate, their lack of decision making is also questioned by others.

Another issue in Christian organizations is that the majority of the workforce is made up of volunteers. This brings its own particular set of pros and cons. The enthusiasm that volunteers can bring to the organization is fantastic. However, because they have a sense of common purpose and direction, they sometimes feel they know what is best for the organization; it is important for the leader to express what best practice is and what high standard is really required. On the other hand, volunteer feedback is often slanted not in the reality of what is happening but in what volunteers think their leader wants to hear and, as such, will often be couched in words reflecting church culture, positivity, and a desire to be seen not to have failed. It is vital that we get the balance right.

When delegating to volunteers remember the following:

- Make sure the person can do the job.

- The subordinate must have a willingness to do the work and the initiative to get it done.

- Make sure the person has a clear understanding of what he or she has been asked to do (including the amount of time required).

- Make sure the volunteer is clear about when and how he or she needs to report to you. As your church grows, the reporting structure will change as more people take responsibility to lead your teams.

- Make sure you have backup assistance when it is needed. Please don't let a person fail for the sake of seeing him or her fail. A failure will reflect badly on the church.

- Let the person know it is okay to make mistakes, but encourage him or her to seek help where necessary.

- Transfer the work, but continue to check that the subordinate knows what is expected.

- Transfer the authority, and ensure this is communicated up and down the line. Don't expect the subordinate to operate without being given an appropriate level of authority (in keeping with the tasks delegated to him or her). Ensure that there is an acceptance of authority.

- Remain interested in what the subordinate is doing and do not abandon them.

- Make sure there is adequate follow up and accountability in place.

Andrew Carnegie once said, "It is very simple. I am merely a man who knows how to enlist in his service better men than himself."[1] Good delegation will bring countless benefits to your organization: it develops talents and latent abilities; it improves understanding at all levels; it develops a rapport between the senior leader and the subordinate leaders; it improves job satisfaction and morale at all levels of leadership; it eases the pressures on the senior leader and releases him or her to concentrate on the more important aspects of the role; it allows the senior leader to develop new skills; and it allows leaders to identify those who are more able and promote them to bigger roles where they can be even more effective for the kingdom.

Leaders, realize that a failure to delegate will not enhance your personal security but undermine your leadership. You are not a one-man show! However, there are some things that a senior leader should never delegate. You are responsible for the vision and mission of the church, not a subordinate. You should never relinquish team building and should always encourage communication and cooperation. Your role is always to set the goals and the parameters.

Decision Making

After delegation, the most important thing a senior leader needs to do is to learn to make decisions. Good decision making is a major hallmark of effective leadership. There are a number of steps I have outlined below that can help. These may sound complicated and time consuming, but a good leader will often naturally process this list in moments. If it is a really important decision, then sleep on it—nothing is so urgent that a good night's sleep won't help!

- Ensure that you have a good understanding of the situation.

- Ensure you have all the information you need—don't make snap decisions in areas where you have inadequate data.

---

1   Andrew Carnegie, http://www.quoteswise.com/andrew-carnegie-quotes.html

- Consider all opinions before proceeding. There is wisdom in consulting others (especially those who will ultimately be affected by the decision).

- Remember, inaction is a decision in itself.

- Assess the pros and cons of each option available. Using all the information gathered, make the best decision you can. However, don't try to anticipate every problem that may result from the decision. You can only work from the information you have.

- Never make a decision while under stress or while upset or angry.

- Don't drag your feet on smaller decisions. If you have the information, make the decision (putting it off will only add to your workload).

- Don't be afraid of making the wrong decision; you are not perfect, and you are not a fortune-teller. Mistakes are part of our learning process.

- Make the decision and move on.

Summary and Advice Checklist

I could discuss much more with regard to delegation and decision making. I have found it to be an area of trepidation for many leaders! However, if we can learn to delegate and communicate correctly, the problems that do arise should be minimal. My final tips on the matter are below:

- Put in place training sessions.

- Meet regularly with all your leaders.

- Give people opportunities regularly.

- Make decisions—people are looking to you for leadership.

12

Developing New Leaders

Chapter 12: Developing New Leaders

Step Twelve: Develop New Leaders

One of the biggest questions I get asked by church leaders is, "How do I raise up leaders in my church?" I am often saddened to find that the first stumbling block many of these leaders find in their way is their own paranoia that those they appoint to leadership will be better than they are. Think about this, even the best chief executives in the world are not good at everything! They purposefully employ people who are better than them at certain things, for the health and wellbeing of their organizations. If their organizations are healthy, they are doing jobs well. Now the church is the most significant organization on the earth—God's "plan A." As leaders, therefore, we have a huge responsibility to move our own egos out of the way to ensure the church is as healthy as possible.

That being said, the process for raising up new leaders is simple and encompasses three areas:

1. Identification
2. Investing
3. Entrusting

Identifying Your Leaders

Look for influence—leaders naturally influence those around them.

Look for character—leaders must be stable and humble. They should be teachable and have integrity (for example, the local gang leader probably doesn't fit into this category!).

Look for people skills—a good leader understands that people are important and is able to empathize with others.

Look for passion—a leader needs to be passionate about what they do and to do it with energy and drive. It doesn't matter if they are passionate about something outside the church (motorbikes or rock climbing, for instance).

So long as being passionate is in someone's DNA, they will also be able to get passionate about leading people in church.

Look for emotional intelligence and life experience—not just academic excellence (though that does sometimes help).

Look for someone who is articulate - someone who can express themselves,the passion they have will be communicated through speech.

Look for people who are willing to learn and grow.

Investing in Your Leaders

In some ways, leadership can be taught in the classroom; the tools and mechanics of leadership are being taught here! However, leadership training is a gradual process that requires on-the-job training and practical work. Allow upcoming leaders to have access to you, spend time with them, take them away on ministry trips and to meetings, and let them see you in action in various circumstances. Conferences are not the sole answer—they exist to recharge the attendees, not to impart leadership skills (I will discuss this more in a later chapter when I talk about transitioning to the next generation).

Entrusting Your Leaders

An upcoming leader cannot live in your shadow forever. Eventually you need to entrust them with real leadership practice. In his early ministry, Jesus healed the sick, cast out demons, and taught the people while his disciples watched. When Jesus sent out the seventy-two, he watched what they got up to. Finally, after he ascended into heaven, the disciples did the work on their own (although with the Holy Spirit's power, of course!) The process Jesus followed could be summarized as follows:

I do, you watch; you do, I watch; you do.

Your leaders have watched you, so now it's time for you to watch them at work and then release them to do it on their own. It's time to start cutting the apron strings. It is more than likely they will get things wrong from time to time, but they are learning just the way you did.

Chapter 12: Developing New Leaders

Partnership versus Membership

Before I end this chapter, let me say something about the difference between partnership and membership. When a church leader recognizes and develops others into leadership, they should do so by emphasizing the idea that those up and coming leaders, are partners in the vision of the church. In partnership, there is a sense of common purpose and responsibility for the success of church programs.

Recently I was in Malaysia teaching a Master Class and we discussed this point, the whole concept of partnership did not translate very well. The students could not understand the difference and that somehow taking ownership was more some sort of legal transaction and that all members in the church had legal shares in the church.

The way I was able to get round this concept was to say that in this area we were talking about ownership on a spiritual level a heart not a seminal ownership. An ownership of vision, culture and values of the church on a spiritual level.

If the leader of a church just emphasizes membership, then people feel that they just need to turn up. They are part of something but have no responsibility for it.

Summary and Advice Checklist

It is time for church leaders to raise up the next generation! Consider the following:

- Get each department head to identify someone who can be trained to take over for them.

- Do some leadership training. This will mature and develop your leaders.

- Ask your current leaders to spend time with their teams outside of "task" to focus on relationship building. A coffee with your team on a Saturday afternoon or a barbeque could help with this.

- Don't be afraid to look at other church leadership development processes; if something has worked for someone else, it could work (or be adapted to work) for your church.

- Let's remember that not all ideas translate well in different cultures and the idea of partnership is a spiritual and heart one.

- By doing this the senior leader of the church should emphasize partnership in this way, which will then lead to ownership.

13

The Time-Out Bench

Chapter 13: The Time-Out Bench

Step Thirteen: Make Use of the Time-Out Bench

The best thing about the game of basketball, other than the fact that all the players are taller than I am, is that they have a time-out bench. During a game, if the coach sees a player lagging, the coach can take the player out of the game for a rest and send him back on the court later in the game. Equally, if the coach wishes to change tactics, he can swap a player on the court for one from the bench. The coach gets the best from his players throughout the game. Many sports have a substitution bench where players not called into the starting lineup wait for their opportunity to make a difference to the game.

In this chapter, we will explore the idea of having a time-out bench for the ministry leaders and volunteers in our churches. Church is not a sports game, and I am not saying it should resemble one (although one church I've been in recently did resemble a rugby match, but that's another story!). However, I do believe the concept of taking time-outs could do us a lot of good. Sadly, I currently know of only one church successfully using the time-out bench concept.

Many denominations have a sabbatical period for their ministers, when they have served a certain amount of time in ministry they are given 3 or 6 months off over and above their normal annual vacation time. This is good when it is used properly. The time-out bench is a concept that is to be used by leaders for their own teams.

Several years ago, I was invited to speak at a church I'd not visited before. Afterward, I found myself having a very heartfelt conversation with the worship leader. She told me how tired and stale she felt but that there was no one else to lead worship. This pressure, along with her day job and family life, was taking its toll. She felt as though she was letting both God and the congregation down by not being fully in tune with the Holy Spirit. She felt she needed a good holiday! I realized that the first thing she needed to do was raise up an assistant, so when she did go on holiday (or got sick) there would be someone else capable of taking over.

Over lunch with the senior leader, I discussed the issue of leaders getting tired and feeling stale. I asked him what strategies he had in place to cope with this. He looked at me, a little confused, and said he'd never thought about it. He didn't have any policy whatsoever for dealing with the problem because no leader had ever come to him and said they wanted to step down. I suggested perhaps that he put in place a time-out bench for leaders to rest and recuperate after a given time period. Sadly, his response was typical: He felt he could not possibly introduce the idea because it would offend his ministry leaders. He was anxious they would feel as if they were being cast aside. Finally, he explained that God had not told him to do anything of the kind!

I must admit that I found his answer incredibly frustrating because God had given him a vision, a direction, and the ability to raise up leaders to build his church. And I never argue with a person who invokes the "God hasn't told me clause." This pastor had power and influence and had many leaders working under his authority and command. However, when it came to looking after the welfare of his leaders, many of whom were volunteers, he seemed content to abdicate his responsibility back to the leaders themselves (remember, inaction is a decision within itself). The result is that the leader works until burning out or leaving the church, and then another leader is hurriedly chosen to take his or her place. This does not produce a more capable leader; it produces a copy of a copy until there is such a dilution that there is no effective growth, vision, or purpose.

A time-out bench is a very simple way of sustaining your best leaders and keeping them fresh. It tells them they have worth to you and their fellow leaders and that you have a bright purpose for their future.

How Does a Time-Out Bench Work?

First, if you are questioning whether or not God has told you to introduce a time out bench, it's common sense—which God gave you to use; it's also good pastoral practice—which he expects you to use! As a senior leader, you should have a strategy for resting your leaders (such as the time-out bench) as part of your core strategic plan. The value of rest is significant and should be nonnegotiable for you (remember, your values help you achieve your vision—which you will never achieve if your leaders are worn out). As was the case with the worship leader I spoke to, few people will actually go to their senior leader to say they are worn out. Often they fear being perceived as a "problem" or as less spiritual than expected. It's the responsibility of the senior leader to be aware of how people are doing, to teach on the value of rest, and to appropriately communicate the church's strategy concerning it—every leader at every level of leadership needs to know what to expect.

Here is how a time-out bench could operate:

- Ask tired and stale leaders to step down for a period of six weeks. They should attend services but sit in the congregation to receive instead of giving out. Only for more serious cases of burnout and stress would I suggest extending this time period to three months. For the most extreme cases you should revisit the issue at three months.

- All leaders should have someone as "second in command" to take charge during their time-out periods (communicate to both parties that this is not permanent). Communicate well from the start with everyone else the change may affect because doing so will ensure that any issues that may arise can be dealt with.

- The leader on time-out must not interfere during his or her period of rest.

- The leader should continue to attend the leadership training nights (monthly), but only return to other events and meetings after the six weeks.

- After six weeks, there is option to take more time off if either of you feel it necessary.

- It isn't a good idea to go on the time-out bench for longer than three months. In this time, the "second in command" person will have begun to establish an identity and ethos in the department they are running. It would be wrong to then expect this person to step aside, especially if they are doing a great job. However, as long as this person realizes that it is only a temporary arrangement, they will likely be happy to step aside when the time comes.

Checklist—How to Introduce a Time-Out Bench

1. Discuss it with your leadership.

2. If possible, make time-outs part of the church culture from the beginning.

3. It is easier for this to be introduced from the very start of a church plant, but in the case of introducing it in an established church discuss it at a training meeting with all your leaders.

4. Communicate clearly to your leaders so they know what to expect.

5. Let your leaders hear your heart and concern for their physical, mental and spiritual well being.

6. Communicate clearly during each time-out process to all involved.

7. Communicate to your leaders that the time-out is not about their ministry skills or their positions but is all about the kingdom of God.

14

Increasing Your Abilities

Chapter 14: Increasing Your Abilities

Step Fourteen: Increase Your Abilities

Does leaving Bible college and taking your first church mean that you give up on developing your skill set? I was in my first pastorate for less than a week when I came to the earth-shattering conclusion that Bible college had taught me nothing whatsoever about pastoring a church! I didn't understand people. I was single and found it difficult to relate to young married couples. I was clumsy around children, and babies frightened the life out of me. Despite this, I learned to adapt. I took on board the advice my mentors gave me and put into practice what I saw them do. This helped me grow my small church from four to forty in only a few months, and then I grew my youth group from four to seventy over an eighteen month period.

When I went into the business world, I learned very quickly. I realized that if I didn't learn, my business would fail and I would be left in a great deal of debt and unable to look after my young family. I adapted by looking for new avenues to promote my company and opportunities to gain business from my competitors. But I didn't stop there; I looked for better ways to run and manage my company. I hired staff; I also fired staff. I trained myself and took courses that gave me skills to lead my company, with over one hundred staff, forward.

Churches are not businesses. They cannot and should not be compared to large corporations. Though many business principles can be used within the church. However, I am surprised at how many senior leaders fail to take their churches forward. Throughout this book I have already outlined many reasons that I believe contribute to their failure, but there is another reason that I believe is also significant: leaders stop learning and training themselves.

This statement raises several questions, which are certainly worth exploring:

1. Is leadership a result of birth, education, or nurture?
2. Can we discover what and where one is in terms of leadership skills and capacities?
3. What makes one leader succeed when another equally trained, experienced, and educated leader fails?

Birth, Education, or Nurture?

I'm not one of those people who believe that the ability to lead is only an accident of birth. Nor am I a person who believes that education and nurture alone will make you a good leader. I believe a good leader is produced by a combination of these things with intellect and life experience (emotional intelligence) also thrown into the mix. Romans 12:8b tells us that leadership is a gift of God and therefore should be conducted diligently. Remember, it is ministry that builds people but leadership that builds churches. Someone straight out of Bible college or seminary, may be able to grow a church to one hundred people, from his or her personality and ministry alone, but it will be a capacity for leadership that will help this young leader build a church of twelve hundred people.

Leadership Skills and Capacities

I like what John Maxwell calls "the law of the lid. "In order to increase our effectiveness we need to increase our abilities"[1] In other words I believe that one man's ceiling is another man's floor. Church leaders must learn to continually assess where they are in relation to their skills. If they are weak in one area, they can gain knowledge in it in order to grow. The key thing here is awareness—I'm not suggesting that we must become experts in everything. For example, during my business days, I was aware that I was not an accountant or a bookkeeper. Therefore, I hired people to do those things for me. However, I still needed to know how my money was spent and on what. I learned through financial management courses to read a balance sheet, understand the tax laws, and know where I should put my profits to maximize my portfolio. I could also tell whether or not my accountant was trying to "cook the books." In other words, I saw where my weaknesses were and did something about them. I didn't need to become an expert, but I did need to increase my capacity to understand and to lead. Church leaders can do the same! They can attend leadership seminars, have coffee with successful leaders, and even listen to training online. I heard recently about a

---

1   7 John C. Maxwell, *The 21 Irrefutable Laws of Leadership* (Thomas Nelson, 2007). Chapter 1 The Law of Influence. Page 1

pastor who listened to podcasts from successful church leaders to discover what God was saying to them and their congregations. He found it interesting that he often had much in common with them. This pastor began to preach and teach similar material in his own church. He also taught his developing leaders in the same way, and he soon began to see some great results. He didn't try to clone the other leaders but adapted the material to make it relevant for his own community. He was increasing his leadership capacity and skills. Eventually others will look at his success and get ideas from him.

Success or Failure?

Failure is not a word people like to use these days. They prefer more politically correct phrases, such as, "He did not accomplish all the tasks" or "She was unable to achieve the goal at this time." It is unfortunate that some of our churches have been in a state of "not accomplishing or achieving" for decades! Their leaders are often highly educated and well trained with plenty of experience. Perhaps they had some initial success in ministry but have stagnated with the passing of time. Conversely, their colleagues may have had great success. Why is this?

Some leaders succeed when others fail because they understand and are able to handle different levels of complexity within their church. A successful leader can approach any number of difficult situations and through a process of intellectual agility bring meaning to what others see as random or chaotic events. This is what I would refer to as "the law of complexity." As a church grows larger, an increasing number of programs begin. The senior leader spends more time on leading and decision making than he spends on dealing with pastoral issues. In other words, the more complex things become, the more the senior leader directs others to do what he once did. However, because of the senior leader's experience, ability to learn, intellectual capacity, and skills base, he is now more able to deal with the issues of a large church than would have been possible five or ten years previously. It's akin to the difference between the responsibilities of a young lieutenant in the army compared to those of his general. Perhaps unexpectedly, the senior pastor's ministry also benefits when he grows in his leadership role. This happens because although the senior pastor spends less time "doing" ministry, he is increasingly excited at everything God is doing in his church, and this excitement gets passed on to others.

The pastor is open to new ideas and dreams. The pastor doesn't look at the problems; he looks at opportunities to build bridges over them.

Summary and Advice Checklist

Leaders may be born to lead, yet without education, nurturing, intellect, and life experience, they will soon fade and become ineffective. A good leader recognizes his ability and increases his skills accordingly. This is an ongoing process during the lifetime of ministry, which should never stop. Failure to understand and to handle different levels of complexity results in churches stagnating.

Consider the following:

- Set yourself a target of reading one book a month. The books could revolve around leadership or a subject that interests you.

- Don't neglect your own spiritual study and growth.

- Read the Bible from cover to cover at least once a year. It is food for the soul.

- Attend some master classes at your local Bible college.

- Consider working on your business skills by doing a course at your local university or technical college.

- Meet regularly with your mentors and those you look up to in the faith.

15

Stress Is Not Burnout

Chapter 15: Stress Is Not Burnout

Step Fifteen: Remember That Stress Is Not Burnout

Very recently I found myself discussing the issues of stress and burnout over coffee with a group of church leaders. There appeared to be the idea among the group that stress and burnout were one and the same thing. Let me say right here and right now—they are not. While talking with these church leaders, I detected signs of burnout in each and every one of them (though, thankfully, none of them in my opinion was burnt out).

We all experience stress; it is not possible to live a life without stress. There is good stress—a sense of joy, fulfillment, and achievement. There is also bad stress (distress) caused by those extreme negative pressures that intrude into our lives: illness, financial problems, and children (to name but a few). Today, as I write, the church worldwide are seeing leaders and pastors burnout due to the complexities of dealing with a pandemic and all that means to their congregations. I will deal with this topic in Chapter 22.

The pressure of building a large church brings its own particular type of stress. The vast majority of great church leaders I have met are, in my opinion, addicted to stress. Stress drives them and gets their adrenalin pumping! The more of it they feel, the more passionate and motivated they become. These great leaders have the ability to manage their stress levels much better than most, which is a vital distinction between those who succeed and those who do not.

Why Does Church Leadership at Times Appear to Be So Stressful?

There is no single, clear answer to the question of why church leadership sometimes appears to be so stressful. However, over the years, I have come up with a list of pressures found within church leadership that are not usually found in other professions:

1. When a church grows, the senior leader takes on different roles. Confusion arises when the boundaries between these roles become blurred.

2. Administrative overload.

3. There is often a lack of clearly defined boundaries within church life; everybody feels they own a piece of their leader.

4. There is conflict between leadership and ministry. Church leaders need to understand the difference between the two. This conflict can often lead to feelings of inadequacy.

5. There is a disparity between everyone's unrealistic expectations and the hard reality of life in church.

6. There is a sense that tasks are never completed (especially if leaders don't understand number four).

7. The leader may find that he has too much discretionary time, unlike other professions that are more structured, which can lead to identity issues and a lack of self-worth.

8. Far too many church leaders have no close friends.

This is by no means an exhaustive list, and it would be true to say that these things can produce huge stress in all our lives. However, it's our response to stress that is most important. It can mean the difference between a successfully functioning church and a small irrelevant church with a burned out leader.

What Is Burnout?

Burnout is extreme physical and emotional exhaustion. There are many different symptoms, and having one or two of them doesn't mean that you are experiencing it. There needs to be a combination of symptoms to indicate burnout. However, knowing these symptoms can help us to modify our behavior before it is too late.

The symptoms are as follows: decreased energy; not wanting to get out of bed; an inability to shake off cold or flulike symptoms; interrupted sleep patterns; an inability to see a way forward even with minor issues and problems; unusual irritability with people who don't see or do things your way; and cynicism and negativity with yourself, others, work, and the world in general.

Senior leaders are often put on pedestals by their congregations just because of who they are. There is sometimes an unrealistic expectation placed upon them to succeed and have all the answers. Personality also plays a part. Church leaders may be either too goal orientated or too spiritually slack in their leadership, and each can lead to its own set of problems. They are usually acutely aware of the responsibilities they carry for their congregations, but at the same time they are aware that they are only human, just like everyone else. All of these things combined with the symptoms mentioned above can easily lead, if we're not careful, to burnout.

How Can We Avoid Burnout?

Most leaders I know have a spiritual routine: they read their Bibles and pray at the same time every day, they fast regularly—fasting can have positive health benefits—and they set aside time to meditate and to prepare their sermons. But sometimes this to can become stale and monotonous.

The first thing I would advise is to stay spiritually fresh: visit someone else's church to receive new ideas and spiritual insight, or go on a spiritual retreat. I have a friend, a Pentecostal pastor, who often goes on a spiritual retreat with a group of Anglican priests. I have another friend who, twice a year, spends a few days alone in a cell in a Carmelite monastery.

All of these things (and there are lots more) can help a leader stay fresh and in tune with God.

Second, take regular time off. Church leadership is not like other nine-to-five jobs. A senior leader will often work far more than forty hours per week. Create good sleep patterns by getting into the habit of going to bed and rising at a set time each day. Eat a balanced diet (Big Mac breakfasts are not the answer!). I believe in a holistic leadership philosophy that is not based solely on ability, talent, or calling, but also on good eating and regular exercise. The fitter you are, the better you can cope with stress.

Third, don't be afraid of change. If you need to change something in yourself, do it. Change is good!

If you don't have any close friends, make some. You need some close Christian friends from outside your church to relax and have fun with.

Finally, don't be afraid of having fun! Your job is the greatest job in the world. It's a calling and vocation like no other.

Summary and Advice Checklist

To keep bad stress and the symptoms of burnout at bay, you could also try the following:

- Take a sabbatical every five years.

- Have regular family holidays and romantic weekends with your spouse.

- Meet regularly with your closest leaders and give them the right to speak into your life if they see these things in you.

- Keep the small things small. In other words, don't make mountains out of molehills.

- If you are unfit and overweight do something about it.

- Go back and read step thirteen.

A stressed out (bad stress) and burned out church leader is no good to anyone, let alone to the kingdom of God!

16

For Pete's Sake, Get Your Family Life Right!

Chapter 16: For Pete's Sake, Get Your Family Life Right!

Step Sixteen: Get Your Family Life Right!

Current research indicates that in the United States, approximately half of marriages involving church pastors or leaders end in divorce. This equals the divorce rate seen within non-Christian marriages. This is a terrible statistic not only for each family involved, but also for the church as a whole. Therefore, I want to discuss here some of the things I have learned that may help a senior church leader safeguard his or her private life.

First, your home life and your ministry are not separate departments of your church. They are intricately interwoven, and this must be understood. Hiding a shaky marriage from your church leadership will put pressure on you, on your spouse, and on the leadership. Eventually, something will break.

I was once at a leadership conference in Melbourne, Australia. In one private session, the keynote speaker allowed people to ask him any questions they liked. When I asked him, "Do you have any mates (Australian slang for friends)?" He was taken aback. My question was not in line with the others he had been answering. It was his wife who shouted from the front row, "No he didn't, but he has now." The man went on to explain how he had taken over the church from his father after returning from college in the United States. He quickly became so wrapped up in the church that he began to neglect his wife and his young children. He put on weight, the problems began to pile up, and he realized he had no one in the church to talk to about his problems. One day on his way home, he saw some older guys playing basketball. He'd played at college and even considered taking up the sport professionally for a while. He stopped the car and got out to ask about the game, which turned out to be part of an amateur league. The man made a choice to get involved and slowly built up a group of friends outside his church who treated him as one of the guys. He was also able to talk to them—in general terms—about his issues, and their expertise helped him solve some of the problems. His wife noticed the changes: he found he had more time on his hands and could set aside time to spend with his family as well as time for basketball.

Over the years, he had the privilege of leading some of his basketball friends to Christ.

My first point: it's very important that a senior church leader has a life outside of church. If you are only ever with people who see you as their leader, you can't interact the same way as you would with friends—you can't relax.

My second point: family time is very important. Treat your children fairly, and love them equally. They need to know you're there for them if they need you. Make sure that the time you spend with your family is quality time. From time to time, try to carve out one-on-ones with each of your children in ways they individually appreciate. Attend and make, their major sports events, school assemblies, music recitals, etc., a priority. Regular family holidays are also a fantastic thing to look forward to and remember together. Have fun together, and do crazy things that will be remembered and go down in family folklore! As your children grow older, encourage them to get involved in church life. Talk frequently and positively about the church, explaining that leading there is your highest calling and a great honor. If these things are communicated to your family, they will understand when you can't be around, but don't make not being around a frequent event. It's a good idea to sit down with your wife on a regular basis and together look at the church diary to plan the week or month or even the year ahead. Significant sporting events, family holidays, and special outings should be put in the diary on an annual basis wherever possible. Then, when you sit down with your leadership team to plan church events in the year ahead, you can plan everything around each other (with some give and take on both sides).

My third point: spend private quality time with your spouse. Do not keep your church problems from him or her. Feel free to discuss them together, and listen to their insight into the situation. Pray as often as you can together—your spouse is just as much a spiritual person as you are and is as much a part of your ministry as your preaching or leadership may be. Share your dreams, thoughts, and ideas for the future with your spouse.

This will envision and excite him or her for what is ahead. Try to go away together at least four times a year, not just for birthdays and anniversaries but also for romantic getaways. Keep the intimacy flame alight! Husbands ought to be proactive in this area and not always rely on the wife to organize things. Your spouse is your greatest friend, and the development of real friendship takes work!

Summary and Advice Checklist

Too many church leaders try to do too much alone without a friendship base or the support of their spouse. The results are always disastrous. Without a hobby to help clear your mind and relax, without friends (both Christian and non-Christian), and without a supportive spouse beside you, you will end up with unnecessary stress and burnout and could even lose everything.

- Ensure your family life is organized and well planned.

- Work with your personal assistant and leadership team in programming church events so they don't conflict with family life.

- Encourage and watch your children grow in their own ministry within the church.

- Love your spouse, and keep the romantic flame alive.

- Get a hobby.

- Have friends outside of church.

17

Transitioning to a New Generation and Making Changes

Chapter 17: Transitioning to a New Gen & Making Changes

Step Seventeen: Learn How to Transition to a New Generation and Make Changes

A short while ago, I attended a meeting made up of leaders from different denominations. It was great to see the way they interacted with each other, comfortable in the knowledge that there were no ulterior motives underlying; no one was trying to steal someone else's flock or seeking to assert one viewpoint over another. No one was Pentecostal, Methodist, Baptist, Anglican (Episcopalian), or Catholic; everyone saw himself or herself as Christian. It struck me that every key leader in this group was over the age of sixty. Only two people, out of a group of forty people, were under the age of forty. Perhaps the comfort and ease surrounding this gathering of leaders came about because they all realized, at their age, they had nothing to lose.

Why is it that leaders find it so difficult to raise up young men and women who will one day take over from us? I have already stated that a key component in healthy church growth is the identification and training of new key leaders; this includes people who are still in their teens. I know of a large and rapidly growing church in New Zealand that identified this problem. Around fourteen years ago the senior leader saw the need to raise up a young leader who could take over from him at the appropriate time. Three young men in their late teens were identified. Two of them did not stay the course and have gone their separate ways into different ministries. On my last visit to New Zealand, a number of months ago, I was thrilled to see that the remaining young man and his lovely wife had been brought onto the leadership team and were beginning to operate under the watchful eye of the senior leader. The vision of the senior leader for the future of his church has resulted in a fresh face and new ideas and concepts being introduced in his church.

It's often said that people, in general, don't like change and are not open to it. I disagree with this! I believe that people do like change. That being said, they do not like it when change is foisted on them suddenly or when there are too many changes happening too quickly. If change is explained to people, and if they understand its necessity, they will usually accept it and move forward positively.

It is essential they can see the leadership team embracing the change with unity. When people see the result is good, they will more readily accept the next changes to come along and life becomes a little easier for the senior leader.

A few weeks ago, I visited a church with a congregation size of about 350. It had remained that size with minor fluctuations up and down for the last ten to fifteen years. I was asked what I would do if I took over as senior leader (a difficult question because I have no intention of entering pastoral work, but it was an interesting scenario nevertheless). In my response, I explained that the most significant thing I could do would be to identify and recognize a young leader to take over from me in the future. I would give the church ten years: after five, I would bring onto staff a young person who I'd been mentoring and developing, a person in their mid to late twenties. Then, after a further five years, I would step aside as senior leader and let the young person take the reins. I would remain for a short while longer, maybe another two or three years, as a father of the house. My role would be that of a senior advisor and mentor, but all major decisions would be made by the new young leader or leaders.

If I was younger, of course, this would not be the case, but I recognize the need to stay relevant to the congregation and the community. It would be irresponsible of me to try to hold onto something because I cling to the past. God always encourages us to move forward. The transition to change in this instance is a long one, but from the very beginning the plan is put in place to make it happen.

Leaders often take over churches thinking they have a job for life. Unfortunately, life moves far too quickly, and before long, they find themselves with a small irrelevant congregation with no plan for the future. Such leaders forget that Jesus took twelve men and over a period of three and a half years trained them to take forward a message to every corner of the globe. Such leaders forget they are fulfilling a calling and a vocation, not a job, and that God is in control. Their role is to ensure that the right people are in relevant positions of leadership at all times and to look after and nurture every generation in order to ensure the future of the church.

Chapter 17: Transitioning to a New Gen & Making Changes

Summary and Advice Checklist

When making changes in leadership and when transitioning to a new generation, you should always have a plan. Spend time explaining things to ensure that people are on board and as convinced as possible. During the process of raising up a new leader to take over from you, spend plenty of time mentoring and developing him or her. Take him or her to senior leadership meetings, allowing the person to listen and take on board the bigger picture. Listen to the new ideas and concepts he or she will have—they will benefit the church in the long run and encourage the young leader. Recognize your young leader's weaknesses and help them eradicate these. Above all, make it clear at all times what the boundaries are and that this person is not in charge yet. Make it clear what the outcome will be, and do not offer false hope, which will only instill disappointment and a lack of trust.

Consider the following:

- Make transitioning to the next generation part of your strategic plan.

- Take a look around your congregation and see what potential is within.

- Make your intentions clear to your leadership.

- Always make your intentions clear to the person you are considering—never give half the picture.

Let us all raise up a vibrant, relevant, and a well-trained new generation of leaders for Jesus.

We have everything to lose if we do not!

18

Church Is a Reflection of Your Story

Step Eighteen: Recognize That Church Is a Reflection of Your Story

The church itself, her physical entity, the bricks and mortar that we seem to invest so much in, reflects who we are and what our story is. Let me explain.

I believe that the way we present ourselves, the way we engage with people, the buildings we occupy, and even the music we play tell people who we are and what we represent. If our church building is old, run down, and in need of repair, we present the image that we are likewise! If we are a "pew and hymn book" church, we may be unwittingly presenting ourselves purely as a people of tradition with no desire to engage with today's society. Perhaps our church uses a data projector, drum-kit, and a sound system, and yet still sings songs written fifteen or twenty years ago. What are we saying to people? Are we saying that we have found our niche and have no need to learn anything new? Are we saying that we have arrived?

There is no better demonstration of this than the way the senior leader uses the physical reality of the church to express his story, vision, and culture. In many ministries throughout the world, we can see this dynamic worked out positively and effectively. Hillsong Church, in the northern west suburbs of Sydney, Australia, is built around the story of Brian and Bobby Houston. Hillsong reflects the vision and culture that the Houston's believed possible. They project a vision for a young, contemporary church, and they hold fast to the belief that the message of Christ is significant and relevant to the world today. Brian Houston has often said that the message stays the same (and has for two thousand years), but the method by which we present it must change. Hillsong present this message in many ways, through its music or its television channel, but another example is the auditorium they have built. It is modern and up to date. It expresses a vibrant culture and the value of excellence. It demonstrates that Christianity is relevant and that the message of the cross can be presented in new and significant ways. Today Hillsong Church is a church of influence in the nation of Australia and beyond. Its idea and vision may have started in Brian Houston's front room, but the vision was not to stay there.

The vision was to build a proper venue that would reflect the big things that God is able to do.

I would like to put forward the idea that one of the reasons for lack of growth in some churches is a problem with the very buildings they occupy. Perhaps these places were once excellent venues, but time and decay catches up with everybody and everything. These buildings no longer communicate the vision, demonstrate the culture, or tell the story as the senior leader would wish to tell it.

How then can we fix this? I am not a design expert, but the basic things I suggest we consider include the following:

Are people comfortable, not only in a literal sense, but in the atmosphere projected within the room? The atmosphere is about much more than padded seats! I have been in some churches where the wooden pews are hard and uncomfortable (more so when the preacher preached for over an hour and a half). However, I have also been in churches with padded seats where the preacher still preached for an hour and a half, and I still felt uncomfortable! The problem was not the chair; it was the atmosphere. I have been in churches where the whole auditorium was enclosed by black curtaining,(for sound proofing purposes) but there was a sense of being cozy and safe. I have also been in churches where there was no curtaining, and I still felt safe and secure. I have been in churches where the lighting was turned down during the worship and turned up again when the announcements were given or when the Word of God was preached. I have been in churches where the music was loud and young people have stood at the front with raised hands and eyes closed worshiping a living and relevant God. I have even been in churches where they have used a smoke machine! The point is this: it's not the design but the atmosphere that counts. Is God there?

How big is the auditorium? Do people feel cramped and feel as though their personal space is being impinged upon? If your church is 80 percent full, people will begin to feel as though they are in a cramped space, and growth will be hampered. Design your auditorium to reflect future growth where curtaining or walls can be easily removed when required.

Chapter 18: Church Is a Reflection of Your Story

If you use lighting and high-tech sound systems, ensure they are operated by well-trained people. Also, your platform needs the right proportions. It should not be too high or too big to accidentally (I hope) convey the message that it is more important than the congregation. However, a platform needs to be large enough for events to work comfortably and for the worship team to grow and move around. The pulpit should be movable—a fixed pulpit can be an eyesore and detract from what is happening on the platform. My personal preference is for a Perspex and chrome lightweight pulpit. It is important you do not neglect your foyer; it is where people get their first impression of the church. If they like what they see in there, they will be more receptive to what they see and hear in the auditorium.

Do you have a well-organized and trained team of ushers who are efficient and friendly? Are they enthusiastic and willing to serve? The hearts of these people, who are your front line for every church event, reflect the heart of the senior leader. Church doesn't start when the first song is sung but in the parking area and at the front door. An enthusiastic welcome is a fantastic first impression.

The auditorium, platform, and pulpit; the sound and lighting systems; the decor; and the teams who make the programs happen are all a reflection of the senior leader. They are the result of the vision and culture of the senior leader being outwardly transmitted. Do not be diverted or intimidated by minority parties within the church who only want their own agendas fulfilled.

Summary and Advice Checklist

If we want our churches to grow, even our buildings need to reflect our vision and culture. The church is a reflection of the kingdom of God, not a reflection of the local pub or nightclub. It's amazing what a simple lick of paint and some fresh thinking can accomplish. Try doing the following.

- Move to a modern facility if possible (the land your old building sits on may be worth a lot of money to a developer).
- If the above is neither possible nor feasible, then put in place a plan to upgrade, renovate, and modernize your building.

- Have regular "work days" at the church building to keep it clean and fresh.

- Think about rearranging or altering your platform.

- Remember, it's all about people; a modern or newly renovated premises will not function without well-trained people.

- None of this will help, if the message of Jesus and him crucified for the sins of the world, is not being preached.

19

Preaching Love, Life, and Purpose

Chapter 19: Preaching Love, Life, and Purpose

Step Nineteen: Preach Love, Life, and Purpose

How and what to preach is very important to any aspiring senior church leader. It is extremely important to get the words right, or the central theme of a message will be lost. A church leader exists first and foremost to tell people God loves them and that he sent his only son to die on their behalf. The words he or she speaks should encourage, edify, and exhort. Preaching life and purpose gives people direction and a sense of belonging in an ever-fragmenting world.

Quite a few years ago, the company I worked for transferred me temporarily to another city. While I was there, I attended a church with a congregation of 150 people, which had previously been much bigger. The senior pastor left most of the preaching to his assistant—a former judge.

Over the next six months, I saw the congregation dwindle to about twenty. The reason for this was simple, every Sunday morning this man would preach death and destruction on all sinners. It felt rather like being shot at dawn and then hung and thrown off a cliff for good measure!

He told us what was wrong with our lives but never told us of the love and mercy of God. His preaching was like a summation in his former courtroom where he handed out judgment with great formality.

I attended another church for a short while where the preacher would usually do a series of sermons. Unfortunately, the core teaching within his messages was lost because the series themselves were far too long (sometimes ten or eleven weeks). The first thirty minutes of each sermon was spent recapping the previous week, and the next forty minutes delivered the next installment.

There was no life in his words or his presentation. An extreme example, I know, and yet it is a familiar scenario in many failing churches. These are two examples on how not to preach!

Below I have listed a number of questions (in no particular order) that I have been asked by young preachers on the topic of preaching:

How Long Should I Spend in Preparation?

This varies and depends on whether it is a one-off sermon or a teaching series. If it is a series, you will need many weeks. If it is a one-off sermon, then at least fifteen to twenty hours in research and preparation will be required, and much more in prayer.

How Long Should I Preach For?

The average attention span of a grown adult is ten to fifteen minutes. Some of the best sermons I have heard (and remembered) have also been the shortest. I would suggest you preach for around thirty minutes, or thirty-five minutes at the very most.

Should I Practice My Sermons?

Yes, of course! I go over my sermons in my head several times before they are preached. However, don't overdo it; you are not a celebrity or an actor. I met one preacher who practiced every sentence and every hand movement and step. I got the impression as he preached that he was looking at himself in a mirror, rather than looking at the congregation. All this made the sermon sound and appear contrived.

What Should I Preach?

Although not every sermon is about salvation and repentance, I do believe there should be opportunity after every service for people to give, or rededicate, their lives to Christ. Jesus is central to our mission to reach a lost world. Also, if you are planting a church, you must repeat your vision, culture and values often in your sermons so that people in the congregation can hear your heart. Principles for life should be taught. The church is the light of the world, so do not be afraid to preach and teach on topical issues (if they are relevant to the lives of your congregation). Topics might include marriage and family, right living, sexuality, giving, how to pray, how to read God's Word, and how to reach the lost (to list but a few).

Should I Let Others Preach?

If you are planting a church you should be very possessive of your pulpit.

When the time comes that you feel another leader can closely reflect your heart for the church and preach the vision, values, and culture you have instilled, you can gradually become less so. If you have taken over an established church and receive a phone call from an itinerant preacher who would like a date to come and preach, then disappoint them by saying no!

How Should I Preach?

This is a very broad question. The simple answer is to practice what you preach. Live it out, and people will see it reflected in your life. Don't preach on sacrificial giving if you have never sacrificially given! We all have different personalities, but even an introvert can communicate life and experience in a relevant, vibrant manner. Someone once said of preaching, "If all else fails then use words."[1]

Should I Use a Text?

Yes, always! The Bible should always be your first port of call for a sermon, not your last. Your teaching should always be Bible-based and well illustrated. I would suggest that we use the New Testament as our main text and use the Old Testament to tell stories and to illustrate human life-its successes and failings.

Should I Tell Stories?

Stories and illustrations fire the imaginations of your listeners and help them apply your core teaching to their lives. The Bible should be your first source, then your own life experience, and lastly the experience of others. If you have a three-point sermon, give three stories or illustrations. Don't waffle, but get to the point.

Should My Preaching Be Designed to Build Attendance or the Attendees?

First and foremost, the mission of the church is to go into all the world and preach the gospel. In the light of this, you should be constantly encouraging the congregation to bring new people to church (where an opportunity to respond to the message of Christ

---

1   The person must have been quoting John Kenneth Galbraith, who first coined this phrase.

will be given after every message). The "building up" of attendees can be done through other programs in the church. Never forget your mission and calling. Doing so will result in the church going into lockdown as you shut out the seeker and the lost.

Should I Do All the Preaching in a Series? And How Long Should It Be?

By all means do this, but don't let a series go for longer than four weeks (the exception to this would be if you are going through a whole book of the Bible). A four-week series, with a morning and an evening service, allows you eight opportunities to preach on the chosen subject. If you have assistant pastors, give them the opportunity to preach on the topic, but always ask for a copy of their sermon several days beforehand to ensure you're happy with it.

Summary and Advice Checklist

Clear, concise, and vibrant preaching that is relevant to our communities is vital if we are to grow large churches. However, although we may work to create an atmosphere for God to operate, it is him, not us, who adds to the church. Without constant prayer and the intervention of the Holy Spirit, our words could be null and void.

Try some of these ideas:

- Have a preaching calendar. Know what you want to preach and teach your church for at least a year ahead.

- Know your subject matter. Ask a young intern or Bible college student to do some research for you. This will save you time and also help him or her gain knowledge.

- Use technology. PowerPoint is a good option if you are doing a teaching series, or the Scriptures you are using can be projected to keep everyone on the same page. Use it sparingly though, many people today are visual learners, they need to learn to use their imaginations.

Enjoy preaching and teaching, and let your face show it!

20

The Weird and Wonderful World of Sunday Morning

Step Twenty: Understand the Weird and Wonderful World of Sunday Morning

The Sunday service is the shop window that displays who we are and the God we represent. I believe passionately that a church stands or falls on the excellence of its Sunday morning service.

I have already discussed the need for the buildings we inhabit to reflect the vision and culture of our senior leaders. I have also discussed the need to get our preaching right. These two things are essential to the way the church is perceived. This same is true of our church services.

I am reminded of the story I alluded to in chapter 1, where my friend bemoaned the fact that he didn't see much of the Holy Spirit in today's church meetings. I can sympathize with him, but what he actually wanted was preaching (mostly about the end times) for over an hour; prayer lines for healing; other gifts of the Holy Spirit in evidence; country and western gospel music; twenty minutes of prayer for people to commit their lives to Christ; and ten minutes of announcements! Usually his own church started five minutes late and ran overtime by ten or fifteen minutes. It is no wonder that he has only twenty-five people in his congregation and that they still meet in the front room of his home.

My friend has forgotten that church is made up of five essential elements:

1. Christ: he is our only constant and total devotion. We must be devoted to him twenty-four hours a day, seven days a week—not just on a Sunday Morning.
2. Commission: going into the whole world is a cooperative and ongoing mission with the Holy Spirit, not just a Sunday morning event.
3. Connectivity: who we make part of our lives and who we connect with through the workings of the church matters.
4. Accountability: it is important for Christians to connect with other Christians. The Bible says, "As iron sharpens iron, so one man sharpens another" (Proverbs 27:17 KJV). Church is about the people who attend, the congregation.

5. Celebration: it is our highest priority to come to worship Jesus.

The mistake many churches make is to try and incorporate all of these elements in one Sunday Morning service. There is too much content and no real focus. We must realize that church is much bigger than the Sunday morning gathering; we represent Christ, who is the center of our lives, throughout the entire week. Everybody ought to be excited about bringing people to church to meet others within a Jesus-centered culture and to celebrate and worship the living God. During the week, those same congregation members meet and connect with one another. They meet needs, pray together, encourage, and minister to one another through the Word of God and even lead others to Christ through work in the community.

The Sunday morning service cannot possibly achieve all of this; rather, it should play its own specific role in the bigger picture of church life. It should be a place we are happy and excited to bring nonbelievers into. When most people think of church, they imagine cold auditoriums, bad acoustics, stained-glass windows, boring liturgy, and terrible preaching. When instead they encounter an excited group of people who see church as vibrant and celebratory, it's a great surprise to them.

Sunday morning services should be no longer than ninety minutes. Many people work six days a week and want to spend Sundays with their families, and this should be respected. To help keep to a reasonable time, you can use a detailed run sheet. As discussed previously, try to keep your sermon around the thirty-thirty five minute mark (a well-crafted message exploring relevant issues will be welcome). Christ-centered praise and worship should be presented with contemporary music and should also not exceed thirty minutes. This leaves twenty five minutes for the welcome, prayer, praise reports, announcements, offering and most importantly, an invitation for non-Christians to commit to Christ.

Take every opportunity to point people to Jesus. Even in the notices and announcements, he must be praised at every opportunity. Don't neglect the section of time before and after the service either;

visitors should be welcomed and invested in. All in all, your Sunday service should be a celebration of Jesus Christ.

Summary and Advice Checklist

- Make a conscious effort to make Jesus the center of your Sunday service.

- Run your service like a well-oiled machine: use a run sheet, and have copies ready for others so that everyone knows what they are doing and how long they have to do it in.

- Mount a clock on the back wall to help keep everyone on track. Also, have a countdown clock to keep the preaching on track.

- Hold a short briefing with all your volunteers before the meeting. This is a fantastic opportunity to spread culture, pray for the service, and enthusiastically center it all on Christ. Your enthusiasm will rub off on those present and then in turn upon the visitors who arrive.

- Debrief each service afterward with those who have played a prominent role. This should not take more than five minutes, remember people have families to get home too.

- Try to speak to as many people as possible after the service.

21

I Am Your Servant, Not Your Slave

Chapter 21: I Am Your Servant, Not Your Slave

Step Twenty-One: Remember That You Are a Servant, Not a Slave

The senior leader of any organization is required to work hard. However, in many failing churches, the demands placed upon the senior leader seem to drift into the realm of the impossible! Their success is often based on the following criteria: Is the leader performing well pastorally? How many people do they counsel? How many of the congregation members are visited each week? Are the sick regularly prayed for? What about hospital visits? Are missionaries being supported? Are the kids and youth programs being run properly, and are they well supported? Is the preaching of good quality? How many people does the leader bring to the Lord each week? On top of this, a senior leader has progress reports to complete for the board, elders to placate, children to be disciplined, marriage counseling to run, and sermons to prepare. He or she must also fit in time for his or her own family, conduct a totally transparent private life, and still be on time for absolutely everything. For all of this, the church will happily pay the senior leader a pittance and maybe provide a manse to live in. After all, it's for "the Lord's work!"

In contrast to this, I have observed that senior leaders who are growing vibrant, relevant, and successful churches also work incredibly hard. Some of them worked up to sixty hours every week when they were first establishing their churches. However, as their churches grew, they raised up leaders to help carry the load. These senior leaders never seem to run out of energy, although everything they do appears to be at full speed. Each day, each project and each department in the church is treated with the same enthusiasm and vibrancy. People are drawn to these leaders, and they in turn catch the leaders' hearts and run with the leaders' vision. There is excitement and life in these churches. People are engaged with people in real lasting friendships, not just the regular chitchat of a typical Sunday morning. They do real life together. All this extends from the hard work of the senior leaders and their teams.

What is the difference between the two scenarios I have just given? Why do 45.5 percent of pastors in the United States suffer burnout within their ministry and feel they need to take a leave of absence? Research also indicates that 75 percent of pastors have had at least one stress related crisis. 24 percent would gladly take another job if they were trained. 13 percent are divorced and 48 percent consider ministry is hazardous to family life.[1] Sadly some pastors do commit suicide.[2]

To my understanding, the answer is simple: it comes down to attitude. Someone once said, "Your attitude determines your altitude." It's one of those feel good, fuzzy sort of statements that life coaches or even mega church leaders sometimes make at conferences to get a cheer from their audience. While it's not a statement I would use, there is an element of truth in it. Our attitudes toward church growth, for example, can result in success or failure. In the first example, it was the response of the senior leader to the attitude of their congregation. In the second example, it was the response of the congregation to the attitude of their senior leader. Both types of senior leaders served their congregations, but the first one was also a slave.

The difference between a servant and a slave is ownership. A servant owns the job or position they are in, but a slave is the one who is owned by the position. A servant determines their own pace, but a slave master determines the slave's pace. The Bible tells us that before Christ, we were slaves to sin (sin owned us). However, the Bible also tells us to serve one another, and to do acts of service (Ephesians 4:12).

In my early ministry, I suffered burnout. This was due in part to the fact that I did not know the difference between a servant and a slave. I thought because I worked for the church I had to attend every single meeting. I worked for six days and nights and rarely rested on the seventh. When the phone rang, I always answered it.

---

1   H.B. London, Jr. and Neil B. Wiseman *Pastors at Greater Risk* (USA Regal,2003) pages 171,21,62 and 86.
2   http://www.crosswalk.com/blogs/christian-trends/why-are-so-many-pastors-committing-suicide.html. http://www.charismanews.com/opinion/watchman-on-the-wall/42063-why-are-so-many-pastors-commit-ting-suicide

Chapter 21: I Am Your Servant, Not Your Slave

When I was told to go somewhere, I always went. If I was treated with disrespect or couldn't pay my bills and didn't eat properly, I took it as my lot in suffering for the kingdom. I was a slave to other people and to what they expected of me.

A successful senior church leader takes ownership of their position. They will instill vision in others so they too can take ownership of it and share the load (see the previous chapter on delegation). The expansion of the kingdom requires us to work with one another, not to work alone. A well trained leader will see the signs of burnout and a slave mentality in their team and will know how to deal with it.

Summary and Advice Checklist

The success of the early church was not based on a slave mentality (though many of the early Christians were slaves), but on a desire to serve one another with the shared aim of spreading the gospel. I believe that if we work together with the right attitude from both pastoral leadership and congregation, the appalling statistics I shared earlier will be greatly reduced or even eradicated. We will see more churches growing, remaining vibrant, and making a real difference in their communities.

Consider the following:

- Are you a servant or a slave to your congregation?

- Does your congregation have an attitude of serving, or does it expect you to meet all its spiritual needs?

- Love everybody.

- Tell your congregation, "I am your servant, not your slave." Ask them, "Will you help me serve?"

22

Leading in Crisis

Chapter 22: Leading in Crisis

Step Twenty Two: Learning to Lead through Crisis.

Thankfully through the years I can honestly say that I have had to deal personally with a crisis only about half a dozen times. I have, on the other hand, had to help a number of Christian leaders through the process of learning to lead in and through a crisis. When dealing with a crisis it isn't just about eliminating the problems but also on how to see and recognize the opportunities that the crisis may present.

Not long ago, I was having coffee during a mentoring session with a young pastor. He told me that he had just been appointed the youth pastor of the church he was now in, when a few weeks later the senior pastor had been dismissed for moral transgressions. He had been appointed by the elders as senior pastor.

The young man told me that the fallout from this crisis was rumbling on in the background and every time he suggested something it got harder and harder for him to control: The ex senior leaders wife wanted her son to take over the church, after all she and he ex husband had planted the church. One of the elders felt that the young pastor wasn't being firm enough with the wife and son of the ex pastor. The young pastor felt that congregation members were talking behind his back and he also felt that he was not getting enough support from the head office of the denomination he was part of.

From his manner I could see that the young pastor was floundering so I offered a number of suggestions that I thought would help him and also help him think more clearly;

1. Separate the perceived threats from the real ones. The worst thing that could happen would be that the ex pastors wife could leave along with her son. Remember you were not appointed by her but by the elders or leadership of the church.

2. Ambiguity is a source of anxiety and needs to be reduced. Get clarification from head office as to what they have done and what they are doing to help you through this crisis. Using this information make a plan. Then approach all your elders and find out what they are thinking.

Leaders can reduce uncertainty by clarifying what changes are in scope. In other words a clear understanding of your point of view will be made, using your information from head office and listening to the wisdom coming from the elders.

3. Inspire confidence by being calm in your decision making and presentation. Armed with your agreed plan it is now time to bring it to the congregation. At the start of the service invite your congregation to remain behind after the service as you have an important statement to make. Immediately after the closing prayer invite people to remain seated. Once everyone is settled bring an outline of what has happened and what has been done to date, inform the congregation what you and the elders are doing and what you will be doing going forward. Invite people to ask question after the service over coffee, invite your elders to stand with you so that you are not the only one being questioned.

This tale does not have a happy ending. The young pastor did not do what I had suggested. The problems brought about by the crisis bubbled on for months, it was the centre of every conversation and every decision. The young pastor could not move forward, eventually he left the church and is now a long distance truck driver. Most of the elders and their families left the church and the wife and son of the disgraced pastor now run the church.

The year 2020 has been a year of crisis, the like of which have not been seen in over a century. The caronavirus, Covid 19 has decimated many communities and has forced the church to do things very differently. Few churches meet face to face as it were, most do online services every Sunday through various social media platforms.

Pastoral work is difficult and many ministers have struggled to put together a coherent plan.

Here are a few suggestions on how to lead through a crisis and may help you in formulating a plan not just for this crisis but for any major church changing crisis:

Chapter 22: Leading in Crisis

1. Think long term: This particular crisis, that we are all involved in at the moment, will go on for many months, if not years. Think about work habits, staff redeployment, new resources that may be needed over the months ahead. A plan can always be altered, but it is always good to have one.

2. Think beyond just your congregation: This crisis may not only effect your congregation but your community. Make sure parish and town officials know that you are there ready to help or co-ordinate wherever needed.

3. Make sure that the message is consistent: Make sure that your staff and leaders are all speaking from the same hymn book. There is nothing more demoralizing for staff, congregation or community to hear inconsistencies and lack of clarity coming from their leaders.

4. Look for new ways of working: Who would have thought that congregations would meet online every Sunday, but many of us do. Having said this, it is important to look for new ways of doing things to try and keep things fresh. People are already beginning to feel "Tech fatigue".

5. See this crisis as an opportunity to re-prioritize on what is important: Normal business will not resume anytime soon. Now is the time to look at those things you have forgotten and may have even neglected. It is time to make people the centre of your focus once again. The church needs to be a place of refuge, shelter and calm in a crisis ridden world.

Postscript

Postscript

The various steps I have suggested take a long time to develop within a church structure. It's called cultural development. It is made a little easier if you are one of the fortunate people who have planted and pioneered a church, because that means your church has your imprint from the start. However, within a five-year strategic plan, these things (and much more) can be accomplished. When I first went into business for myself, within the construction/project management field, it took me a short while to find my feet. After a settling-in period, I put into operation a five-year business plan. Every year, I revisited it and adjusted things, but all the time I aimed for the goals that I had set in my plan. I reached them and then set a new five-year plan to fulfill. This time I reached the goals I set for myself in three years—I was learning all the time. It should be the same with your church.

Within the first three to six months, vision, values, and culture should have very quickly been laid down. This is done through preaching, teaching, and constantly speaking into the lives of your leaders. Your first eighteen months to two years should be clearly laid out with specific and achievable goals outlined. After your first strategic plan, a five-year plan needs to be developed. There should be a reasonable amount of flexibility for change within the plan as and when it is needed, but the plan should only be changed for a solid strategic reason.

From the beginning, you need a process by which you take young converts right through to strong discipleship. In the same way, you also need a process to train and develop your department leaders. Ensure that you have a leadership meeting at least once a month and have a leadership retreat once a year in a venue other than the church. There are some who would say that this should be an evolutionary process; as departments grow, the need for and the development of leaders will take place naturally. This is partly true, but good leaders have the ability to see further down the road. Good leaders can preempt potential situations where leadership gaps might be created by providing good training ahead of time to emerging leaders who will, therefore, be prepared to fill the gaps as required. The evolving idea alone results in a chaotic process and rarely delivers what it promises. However, stable structures developed with good forethought and training will free up the leadership team to get on with the job.

Never be afraid to keep asking for volunteers. The church needs them and can't do without them. It is from your volunteer pool that your future leaders will be seen, recognized, and developed. The old excuse that 20% of the church congregation does 80% of the work is just that, an excuse. It does not excuse your lack of volunteer training nor for not developing a process to raise up young leaders.

Always remember that good, clear, and concise communication is needed at every level and in all situations when dealing with your leaders. I loathe meetings! I find them boring and get particularly frustrated when they veer off on a tangent to debate a mundane issue or irrelevant fact. Keep control of your meetings to keep things on track. Have an agenda and have a time limit! Another idea may be for everybody to stand in a circle for these meetings; that way no one gets comfortable. The people who attend your meetings are usually volunteers with their own work and family commitments. Please respect their time. Also, keep records of every meeting: accurately count those who are there, look for regulars who might be missing (it could be a pastoral matter your team needs to know about), and ask someone to record the minutes for you to review afterward.

Ensure that the financial matters are seen to and that the legal requirements are met by your board of trustees. Your board should include one or two outsiders and both men and women to ensure no particular bias. They should meet four times a year, but you will need to see your financial person at least once every month. You need to know where the money is going and who is and is not tithing (it's particularly important that all your leadership are tithing and giving and are fully committed to the success of the church). An understanding of the monthly finances will help you see trends and know when to ask the congregation for more money or to take up a special offering. While *money*, to some, is a dirty word, your church needs it to grow and succeed in its vision!

Keep yourself fresh by seeking out successful people in ministry who can build into you, teach you, and direct you through difficult situations. Meet with them as often as you can. Look into and examine why they have been successful. I realize this is harsh to say, but do not align yourself with poor or mediocre leaders who have struggled for years and never built anything of significance. Instead, believe that God can and will do big things and that your vision, values, and culture set you and your church apart. Once you are in a strong position, then you can reach out to them and see if they need help.

Set aside time in your yearly calendar to go to conferences. Choose a spiritual one and one that has a great deal of substance. Remember to share what you have learned with your leadership and to consider how it might be applied to your church (not everything will be applicable or easily transferred, but principles are universal). As you grow bigger, take some of your leaders and potential leaders to these conferences.

Take your day off each week to do something different (if possible, with your spouse). If you are a family man, do not neglect your family, and keep them informed concerning what is happening at church. Encourage them at an appropriate age to get involved in church life. Keep your word, and remember to go on regular family holidays and outings.

Do not neglect your own spiritual development, but adamantly set aside time daily for mediation, prayer, and Bible reading—you need to hear from God.

The larger your church grows, the more complex the issues you will have to deal with. You will find that more and more of your time will revolve around issues of leadership instead of ministry. In order to deal with these issues, you will have to understand the limits of your abilities and increase them accordingly. Remember, "One man's ceiling is another man's floor level." Through personal development, you can increase your ability to handle bigger and more-complex scenarios. Time and experience will also help, and your ability to raise up leaders to deal with the bigger and more-complex issues will be crucial.

You have been called to the greatest vocation on earth: to partake in building the church! It is important you have fun doing it. There is nothing worse than a dry and boring senior church leader. Take hold of what God has done for you! Get excited about serving him, and seek to envision, enthuse, and release those around you. What a great calling we have: to lead dead people to life by introducing them to our Lord Jesus Christ!

Postscript

Recommended Further Reading

The L Factor, *The Empowered Church*, and *Re-Engineering the Church* are all by Dr. Ian Jagelman of the Jagelman Institute in Australia. Dr Jagelman has a unique way of approaching the subject of church leadership. You will find his analytical and logical approach refreshing.

On the Psychology of Military Incompetence by Norman F Dixon is also an excellent read.